THE Parent
Fix

THE Parent

Fix

When Parents Change,
Kids Change

MAGGIE STEVENS

Published by Familius LLC, www.familius.com
Familius books are available at special discounts for bulk purchases for sales promotions, family or corporate use. Special editions, including personalized covers, excerpts of existing books, or books with corporate logos, can be created in large quantities for special needs. For more information, contact Premium Sales at 559-876-2170 or email specialmarkets@ familius.com

Library of Congress Catalog-in-Publication Data
2014945905

pISBN 978-193-962-920-3
eISBN 978-1-939629-83-8

Printed in the United States of America

Edited by Amanda Wind
Cover Design by David Miles
Book design by Brooke Jorden

10 9 8 7 6 5 4 3 2 1

Second Edition

Contents

When I Changed, He Changed

The boys on my son's baseball team had played ball together for years and were the best of pals. They cheered together wildly when a teammate knocked a ball out of the park and tormented each other mercilessly when someone struck out. I watched them in the dugout as they chewed on big wads of gum and high-fived each other while they kept up a steady flow of chatter. At the naive age of thirteen, grade school was a thing of the past. They were on their way to middle school. Exuberance for life was evident on their faces. Life was so simple and so good.

As I watched my son step up to the plate, I realized this brief period would soon come to an end. This group of boys would no longer play ball together as a team after this season. Some would move on to a higher level of baseball. Others would drop baseball, eager to pursue different dreams.

Challenges would enter their lives. Girls were becoming interesting, and a variety of school activities would soon pull them apart. The boys did not realize what we, as parents, knew would be inevitable: their lives would head in different directions, never returning to this period of time. They would never be thirteen again. I wanted to tell my son to cherish this moment as it would soon be gone. When the last of childhood melts away, nothing is ever the same again.

The boys had much life yet to experience. They were ready and excited to face whatever new opportunities were presented. As I watched my son, I realized that although he might be ready, I was not. I was not prepared for him to move on. I had this nagging feeling I had not done enough. Was he ready for the experiences he would encounter in the next few years? How would he respond when introduced to alcohol . . . drugs . . . parties . . . truth-or-dare games? At that moment, a terrible thought crossed my mind. *What if he failed?*

Suddenly, the simplicity of the evening at the baseball park was gone. I shut my eyes and said a silent prayer. Was there any way to let him skip this next stage in his life and move into adulthood unscathed? I was ready and willing to try. With those fears racing through my head, I wished I could eradicate those awful teenage years from existence. Deep down, I knew my son had to go through them. The challenges he faced during high school would be the driving force he needed to help him develop. These experiences would mold him into the adult he would soon become. But to think about it was frightening. Again, I wondered . . . have I done everything possible to prepare him for what lies ahead?

My fears were well-founded. Over the years, I had watched as multiple friends lost their teenage children to full scale rebellion. These kids, who were their parents' greatest sources of pride and joy, had now metamorphosed into holy terrors, defying authority, drinking excessively, partying, and ignoring any parental jurisdiction.

When asked what was going wrong, the parents seemed as confused as the kids. When their children refused to respond to their pleas, parents tried counseling. The counseling might solve the problem for a short period of time, but eventually, in spite of their efforts, the same poor behavior adjusted back to the way it had been. There seemed to be one question that resurfaced again and again:

"What have we done to deserve this behavior from our kids?"

This was not how these parents had planned out their lives. They loved their children and felt they had done everything within their power to raise good kids and create a happy home life.

As I watched what they were going through, it frightened me. My dreams of what a family should be seemed impossible. What made me think my life would be any different from that of my friends? Sitting here at the baseball park, I pondered this question. I looked at my son. He was warming up on deck. In his face, I saw an innocence that made me think there had to be a better way. I did not want to lose our relationship. I left the ballpark that evening determined to figure out what it took to be successful at this parenting thing.

In the days that followed, I searched for a plan. I went to the library and checked out books on parenting. I read and read and read. Some of the advice was good, but after trying it on my own children, I found it did not work. I was also surprised to discover that many of the authorities writing these books had never raised children. Did they truly understand what it took to parent day in and day out? The advice they gave sounded good, but the concepts were impossible to implement. I have found that the lessons I learned from real life experiences have been the most valuable to me.

I did not need answers that sounded good. I was looking for someone who knew what they were talking about. I wanted information that worked. I changed my approach, quit reading so much, and began observing parents in action. I watched parents at school functions, church meetings, and grocery stores. I watched every interaction I could between parent and child. I got as close as I dared, close enough for eavesdropping on conversations. At first, it appeared that all the parents I witnessed were struggling with their teenagers. These families did not get along, and they certainly did not enjoy spending time together. It was discouraging to watch, but I refused to give up. There had to be a better way.

I kept watching. The more time I spent observing and analyzing, the more I began to notice differences. Not all parents were feuding with their kids. There were a few, a small few, who were actually enjoying their teenagers. Those interactions were different. In the market, they were not fighting over what they would have for dinner. They were laughing, planning, and making decisions together, throwing both Twinkies and apples into the cart.

At the airport, one family caught my eye. They were in a crowded terminal waiting for a delayed flight. While everyone around them was stressed and was pacing the terminal, this family was spread across the floor, laughing and playing cards. I witnessed a love that exhibited itself in their interactions with one another, a respect that was exemplified in their conversations. These parents were doing something different, and it was working.

This family's kids appeared to be happy and content. The tension I had witnessed in other families was nonexistent. I am sure this family must have had their problems; no family is free of problems. But what impressed me was how they seemed to enjoy being together.

Another family particularly impressed me with how well the parents related to their children. I had seen them numerous times around the neighborhood. I got bold and approached the mother. I am sure I surprised her with all of my questions about her unique style of parenting, but from her answers, I found a mother with confidence in the relationship she had with her kids. She knew what she was doing. I watched as she joked with her daughter about situations and subjects that other parents would never have dared discuss.

She was pleased I had noticed the difference in her family. Of course, she knew there were differences, and she was flattered I would even ask. She challenged me. If I was willing to learn, she would teach me all that she knew. I could see the results this woman was getting from her teenagers, and I needed to know how she was actually doing this. As a young, naive mother, I had no idea what I was getting myself into . . . or the changes that were about to occur in my life as a result. Thus, I stumbled onto my first apprenticeship. During the next few days, she answered all of my questions, giving me every piece of advice I could digest. At times I was skeptical of her unique ideas, but I listened closely to the information she gave me. I tried each of the suggestions she gave me, and they worked!

As I became more comfortable with her advice, I began calling her whenever a problem arose. This mom knew her stuff! She would comfort me when I was stressing over behavior that was normal. She knocked me into reality when my kids were doing things that needed to be changed. *She taught me that my focus should not be on changing my child's behavior, but on understanding the child and figuring out why the behavior was occurring.* The wisdom I gained from this woman greatly improved my life and my family. I will always be indebted to her for her willingness to share her knowledge. My duty now is to pass this knowledge on. If it improves life for even one child, it will have been worth the effort.

An affirmation of these new methods appeared quietly one afternoon as I tuned into a program on talk radio. The topic was teen drug abuse. Many callers phoned in, giving personal experiences, sharing their levels of frustration with their children. Treatment programs or rehab would work for a while, but when the kids moved back home, everything fell apart. Finally, a ray of hope in an otherwise depressingly overcast show broke through the thick clouds. One caller confirmed everything I was beginning to understand. This father shared harrowing experiences involving his drug-abusing son, now in his late twenties. His son had been in rehab numerous times from the age of fourteen through young adulthood at age twenty-eight. Finally, they had reached a new level of success. The host and this father discussed in depth all that had happened between father and son. There was much sorrow and pain interspersed with a lot of love. I cannot quote all that the father said, but I will never forget one sentence:

"*It wasn't until I altered my behavior towards my son that everything finally turned around. When I changed, he changed.*" His statement stopped everything. Even the talk show host was dumbfounded. The airwaves fell silent. The host soon gathered his thoughts and launched into a list of other possible reasons for the change in the young man's behavior. The father stopped the announcer and stated firmly, "*You weren't listening to what I just said to you . . . When I changed, he changed.*"

At that moment, I realized all of my studies, observations, and experiences had culminated in one short sentence: "When I changed, he changed."

I had my answer. I could no longer deny it was I who had the biggest influence on my children's behavior. I was responsible for how they felt about themselves. I was the one who could make a difference in their lives. It was my responsibility—no, my privilege—to teach them correct principles. They needed my protection, my respect, and my love to help them handle the problems they encountered as they worked their way through life.

The problem with today's kids is not the kids—it is the parents. The parents and the way we are trying to parent our children. As parents, we are well-intentioned, but we are parenting our children the wrong way.

Would changing the way I approached parenting be a challenge? Yes, perhaps the greatest challenge in my life, and exactly what I signed up for in assuming parenthood. Learning new methods would take time, practice, and patience . . . a lot of patience. But I was relieved to have the answer I knew was right. I was ready for the task ahead.

Thus, I began my journey towards change. With time, and as I began to understand the concepts, it got easier. I gained confidence in my parenting skills. Over time, I saw changes in my family, changes that came as a result of altering the way I was handling everyday situations. Each time a problem arose, I knew I was capable of solving it. It made me feel powerful. I was in charge of the attitudes that abounded in my home. I now understood my role as a parent.

One prominent religious and community leader, Gordon B. Hinkley, states it clearly:

> I believe our problems, almost every one, arise out of the homes of the people. If there is to be reformation, if there is to be a change, if there is to be a return to old and sacred values, it must begin in the home. It is here that truth is learned, that integrity is cultivated, that self-discipline is instilled, and that love is nurtured.[1]

Parenting can be frustrating. It requires endless amounts of time and hard work. If you really want help with your children, implement the parenting methods in this book. You will be successful. Although the topics in each chapter may seem insignificant or simple, the small adjustments you make as a parent will greatly affect your child. If you can stay open-minded as you read this book, it will change the way you parent. The results you witness in your children will keep you motivated. Watch, ask, read, listen, be flexible, and continually try and test each new method. The results are worth it. I know because it has worked for me.

Troubleshoot

As you begin to comprehend and change the atmosphere in your home, you cannot help but realize the mistakes you have made over the years. Parents try their best, yet all have made mistakes. One does not launch into a project such as parenthood without soon realizing that there will be many errors along the way. You may be overwhelmed with guilt. There is no reason to feel guilty as you read this book. The examples in this book are taken from real families. Because they are true, they will hit close to home. You will recognize yourself in many of the examples, just as I once did. As you read, remember that guilt does not bring about improvement. Guilt will stop your forward progression. As you recognize the mistakes made, forge ahead and make the necessary changes. Don't let anything stop your progress, especially guilt. Even the most conscientious parents have made mistakes. We all fall short of perfection. The discovery that we are responsible for our troubles does not condemn us, but it opens up a way to freedom. Move forward with your new knowledge and build from there. Don't look back. Remember, children adapt quickly. If you change your behavior, you will see your child's attitudes and behaviors change quickly.

When you realize that you are your own opponent standing between you and your child, you will have an easier time knocking down the walls that are blocking the progress in your relationship. As you begin your change, keep in mind the following suggestions:

1. *Be bold.* Commit to the new ideas that will be introduced. Vow that the new idea you have been introduced to *will work.* Humble yourself. Open your mind and your heart and give it a try.

2. *Be willing to assess your current parenting methods.* This means looking at a situation honestly and asking yourself:

    - Is this working?
    - Is my child happy?
    - Is my child motivated?
    - Are we progressing?

3. *Be honest.* Children give immediate and honest feedback. Be forthright and clear so you can honestly evaluate the messages your children are giving.

4. *Worry wisely.* Worrying can be a good thing. It helps you deal with problems before they become disasters. But make it productive worrying. Productive worrying catapults you into action

and brings about positive results. Don't overdo the worry; be positive.

Good luck . . . keep all hands, arms, feet, and legs inside the ride at all times . . . and have fun.

CHAPTER ONE

Safe Haven

Rules of Play

The object of the parenting game is *not* to become the wealthiest player through buying, renting, and selling property. Rather, it is to create a haven wherein parents and children converge to enjoy the simple pleasures of life.

No pleasure in life compares to being a parent. Very few experiences in life will be as rewarding. It is valuable for parents to understand that one fact. First Lady Barbara Bush told the graduates at Wellesley College:

> Whatever the era, whatever the times, one thing will never change: Fathers and mothers, if you have children, they must come first. You must read to your children and you must hug your children and you must love your children. Your success as a family, our success as a society, depends not on what happens at the White House but on what happens inside your house.[1]

As you read this chapter, keep in mind that the most important thing you can give your child is yourself.

We live in a world where many are deceived into believing that possessions are more important than people. The more "properties" we acquire, the happier we think we will be. We compare ourselves to our neighbors. We compare and compete. Most of us conduct our lives with the idea that if we can provide our families with the physical things in life, we are meeting the needs of our children. While financial stability is important, it does not solve our problems. Financial stability will never provide the support that individual love and care will. Buying a bigger home with more space is not the solution to stop the kids from fighting. Going into debt for a new car is not the solution for taking the family on vacation, and while it may impress the neighbors, it will have no effect on your parenting abilities. While we're on the subject, adorning your children with overpriced clothing or the best sporting equipment may not be the quickest road to popularity for them or you. Subconsciously, we believe that physical things will bring peace and stability into our lives. In reality, possessions usually add to the stress. We don't need lots of "things" for our home to be a Safe Haven for us and our children.

Begin by Rolling the Dice

Creating a "Safe Haven" is the basis for family improvement. The Safe Haven is the foundation you will build upon. Constructing a Safe Haven provides the environment that will make it possible for positive change to occur. In the beginning, the Safe Haven is difficult to create, but try not to get discouraged. The formation of this Safe Haven is a process which slowly evolves with dedication and practice.

To understand the importance of this Safe Haven, let me remind you about our culture. Sometimes, as parents, we forget how difficult life is for our kids. We send them out the door, not comprehending all the challenges they will face in a day. They worry about things like fitting in, finding friends that will accept them, attending school dances, doing well in class, passing a test, making a sports team, or trying out for cheerleading.

They may not talk much about it, but they do stress over it. As parents and adults, the challenges we have in our own lives seem insurmountable. It is the same for our kids. It is important not to discount the problems our children have just because they do not seem as important as our own problems.

The world we live in is not a safe place for our children, physically or emotionally. Michael E. Berrett, PhD, president of the Center for Change, explains:

> The culture we are a part of—the culture that we are
> bringing to and leaving with our children—is a culture
> which hurts them. It hurts them because it does not teach
> them that they are good, worthy, valuable, and important.
> It does not adequately teach them that their value comes
> from who they are, rather than the external "what they
> do." We owe it to our children to do everything we can
> to correct the cultural messages which equate success,
> beauty, and goodness only with external appearance and
> accomplishment.[2]

This society our children face every day is filled with cell phones, social media, adult-focused entertainment, stress, and tough decisions. We are throwing our kids into a life that full grown adults struggle with and they are still children. Are we giving our children the patience, the understanding, the time, and the attention they need? Even in the best of homes, we will struggle if we allow this fast-paced lifestyle to continue inside our homes. We must make personal changes and give our children the attentiveness they deserve, or we will witness more abnormal, addictive, and unhealthy behaviors.

So how do we combat this world on behalf of our kids? It would be wonderful if it was possible for us to change society, but that in itself is an overwhelming topic worthy of another book. What we can and must do is control how we let our children be affected by the world. This chapter is important. It is through the Safe Haven that you can direct your child's environment.

Throughout this process, remember that your children don't need to be frightened of the world. Begin by managing or taking control of a small part of your child's world—the home.

When I talk about establishing a Safe Haven, the place to focus your energy is in your home. Home is the place for nurturing and teaching. It is where we have the power to prepare our children to feel good about themselves. If they leave home with confidence, they will be able to effectively handle whatever the world throws at them.

Let me give you a better picture of the environment you are trying to create. In this Safe Haven, your child should feel the world is a friendly place. This is the space where a child can and should be a child. It is here where your child is loved unconditionally. Your home cannot be a place of contention or competition. At home, your child should never be judged or threatened. There needs to be an aura of peace and calm. Patience must be abundant in this home. This is a Safe Haven.

> Kindness is a language which the deaf can hear and the
> blind can see.
>
> —Mark Twain[3]

You, the parent, are the most important part of your child's life. It is imperative that you are present and willing to assist. In your home, there needs to be an abundance of listening—more listening than advice-giving. There is a reason God gave us two ears and only one mouth. When a nonjudgmental and caring atmosphere exists, children feel validated and that their opinion matters. There can be *no* yelling, *no* criticizing, and *no* demeaning, only positive understanding. With that as their base, they will share their feelings more openly.

Your home should be a place where ideas are shared freely. Children need to be encouraged to express their opinions without criticism. In an effective Safe Haven, beliefs need to be discussed openly. In all your conversations, leave the stress outside. Allow your family to feel the warmth that comes from open and understanding conversations.

Love needs to be expressed on a daily basis. Your children must know they are valued and are an important part of the family unit. In this Safe Haven you are trying to create, it is not good enough to merely accept your children—they need to be cherished.

The change to cherishing a child comes from a change in the parent. If there is one single principle that is central to creating a Safe Haven and becoming a more powerful parent, it is to be teachable. To be teachable means to become as a child: accepting, loving, patient, humble, and willing to submit. Who we are affects what we do, so our submissiveness will be reflected in our parenting. If you are teachable, you will learn more from your children than they will learn from you.

There are certain forms of expression that erode the Safe Haven. The most common is fear. It helps to acknowledge that fear is expressed through anger, yelling, criticism, and contempt. You cannot parent effectively out of fear. Negative emotions will make it impossible for the Safe Haven to flourish.

While creating a Safe Haven, I have found it important to continually remind myself that children, especially teenagers, cannot be viewed as little adults. They are children. Often, as adults, we expect more of our children than they are capable of doing. If you can keep this understanding always present in your mind, you will find it easier to parent in an age-respectful manner.

You might be rolling your eyes, thinking, *This Safe Haven sounds wonderful . . . totally impossible, but wonderful.* Please do not feel that this Safe Haven is unattainable. We are all at different stages with our families. No two havens can or will be the same. Our families all have unique dynamics: two-parent families, divorced families, widowed families, large families, small families. However, the principles are all the same. Slowly, step by step, make changes that will improve your home environment. It works. You will be amazed at the changes that can occur within your family by just taking this first step.

Stay focused. Try in every interaction you have with your children to show them that they are valued. From your actions, you will be teaching your children that their individual worth is great. Then they can enter the world with the confidence that they need to succeed.

Margaret McFarland, a well-known child psychologist, expresses how important a loving relationship is to a young child:

> As a child is loved, he loves in return. To understand children, we have to understand powerful human influences or strong impulses conceived in love. It's called "part and counterpart," the interplay—positive or negative—between humans and their intimate relationships.
>
> The nature of this interplay is critical during a child's early years. Things can go very wrong if a child does not receive positive messages.
>
> There is no daycare center that replaces the mother. If in the future children are reared in groups, the human personality will become different.[4]

As you continue reading, I will give you practical solutions on how to get and keep this atmosphere in your home. So before you eschew the idea of the Safe Haven, thinking it is impossible, give it a try. Who knows? You may even land on Free Parking.

Proceed Clockwise around the Board— One Turn at a Time

The best way to begin creating the Safe Haven is by executing one concept at a time. Although quick changes can make you feel like you are rapidly making progress, big leaps should be reserved for those who have no other choice. If you try to clean up all the negatives at once, you will become frustrated or begin to doubt yourself, eventually giving up.

It is imperative to stop the belittling behavior that is occurring in today's families. With verbal abuse on the rise, I strongly suggest this be your first step. Parents must decide that there will be no more screaming, yelling, or demeaning of their children in the home. For the first week, make the commitment and stick with it. Do not speak to your child in a loud voice or with anger. If yelling has become a habit, this first step will be a tough thing to accomplish. Put yourself in control. It will take time, but it is possible to change. This change is important because every time you scream at one of your children, you are destroying a piece of that child's self-esteem.

Change is always difficult, but if visuals work for you, picture this. The next time you start to get angry and yell at your child, picture yourself handing him or her a marijuana joint. I know this sounds harsh, but I want you to understand the serious damage that can occur to your child when you yell. As a parent, you are supposed to love your children unconditionally. Yelling at or criticizing your children can make them feel terrible about themselves. In order to recover, they may eventually find another way to feel good again. Constant demeaning of a child drives them to find another source of happiness. Sadly, drugs and alcohol often satisfy that need and can provide teens with a false sense of happiness, security, and acceptance. This type of destructive behavior happens all too often. Many find it hard to believe that a child's life can be destroyed simply by yelling. Bit by bit, when you demean your child in any way, shape, or form, you are destroying self-esteem. Negative behavior, such as underage drinking, often occurs when a child feels bad about him- or herself. I hope the recognition of this practice will shock you into stopping yourself when you yell or say negative things to your child. Love needs to be the language that is spoken in your home.

Anger, which leads to screaming and yelling, has become all too common in today's families. Stephen Duncan, a professor of family life, helps us to understand anger and has some suggestions for finding constructive ways to deal with anger.

Duncan explains that anger is expressed in three ways, two of them destructive. The first is through outward aggression and the response is explosive. You hit someone, smash something, scream, or yell, exacebating the problem. This way of expressing your anger does no good and actually harms the people around you.

The second negative way to handle anger is by refusing to acknowledge the anger by containing it within. This anger may not harm the people around you, but because it is directed inward, it will be harmful to your health. This method of controlling your anger often causes depression, high blood pressure, or may lead to drug and alcohol abuse.

The third mode of anger Dr. Duncan talks about is the control of anger. Instead of ignoring the anger or acting out, it involves calming oneself and using the anger to rationally solve a problem or achieve a constructive resolution with others. This is the most constructive way to handle your anger.

Dr. Duncan stresses that we are never forced against our will to lose our temper. Anger is a learned response to something that upsets us. The fact that we are angry is not the problem. The issue lies in how we react. You must acknowledge that you have the power to control your anger. Notice how you react. Do you tense up? Does your heart pound? Do you breathe rapidly? Remember you have the freedom to choose how you will react. I believe the best way to handle this is to plan your reaction.

Notice your triggers. Do you get angry when your child breaks their curfew? Is it when your husband leaves his clothes on the floor? Is it when your boss doesn't acknowledge your efforts? Remember you cannot change the situation or the other person, but *you* can change. Don't let your anger exacerbate the situation.

The next step is to plan your reaction. If you know what time your child will be home, take the time to plan out how you will respond. Remember you have the freedom to choose your emotions. Dr Duncan can help you:

> Calm yourself first. . . . [Y]ou must first reduce the inten-
> sity of the angry feeling by calming yourself. Discover
> what methods help you calm down when you become
> angry. Such things might include calling a friend or

relative, listening to music, praying and meditating, exercising, writing down feelings, sleeping, taking a warm bath, breathing deeply, counting to 10, or simply thinking about a peaceful, beautiful place.

[P]arents should learn about children's behavior at different stages of their development and recognize that certain undesired behaviors may be normal for a child at a given age and maturity level. Such knowledge can help a parent respond lovingly when a child pushes an anger trigger. . . . Practice expressing concerns calmly and with an attitude of respect, without attacking or blaming the other person. Explain why you feel angry. Use statements that follow an "I-feel-when-because" format, such as "I feel frustrated when you come home after curfew because that is against our agreement." Follow this up with the change you believe to be necessary to solve the problem.[5]

Even when expressing anger, we can communicate love and respect. With a gentle touch on a child's shoulder and a calm voice, you can communicate that you still care about the child and value the relationship. . . . When anger is recognized and approached calmly, respectfully, and with the intention of strengthening the relationship and not hurting it, it can actually encourage growth and intimacy.

Once you feel the loud outbursts are under control, it is time to tackle another ill-fated practice. This can be one of your choice. Pick whatever value you feel necessary to improve your Safe Haven. If you are struggling to come up with the next step you need to improve, ask your child. I am sure he or she will have no problem deciding what needs to change. For example, you could begin to practice attentive listening. Or you could try verbalizing to your child how valuable he or she is to you. The key is simply to choose one task at a time to accomplish. If, after you move onto a new task, you blow it, lose your cool, and start yelling again, stop. Go back and focus on that concept one more time. Take it slow and in simple steps. Choose your own pace. It will seem impossible at first. But little by little, small changes in the aura that surrounds your home and your child's behavior will begin to take shape.

Examples always help. The following three examples will help you create your Safe Haven.

Sticking to Your Strategy—Example 1

Kathy was a stay-at-home mom. She tried very hard to be a good friend and neighbor. Kathy involved herself by taking dinner to families in need or volunteering at the hospital. She often spent hours on the telephone helping others with their problems. She tried to be a good mother. When her three children came in the door from a day at school, Kathy was always home. She was a great role model of service to her children. Yet, with all of her dedication, something was wrong at home, and Kathy knew it. Her children were not doing well in school and ran with a wild crowd. Kathy could not figure out what had gone wrong. She could help everyone else with their problems, but she was lost when it came to fixing the problems in her own home. With the endless fighting amongst her children, it seemed there was always tension in their home.

Kathy's troubling home life came about because she was not totally present for her own family. She had become so absorbed in the lives of others that she had forgotten to first take care of her own family. Kathy's kids needed their mother to focus on them, to be available when they needed her. Her children required help with their school work. The kids would never admit it to her, but they liked it when their mom was home after school asking how their days went. Kathy had been home, but she was always on the phone and inattentive to the needs of her children.

Kathy knew things needed to change. She also wanted to continue to help other people because she felt good about her life when she was involved in service. Kathy reevaluated how she was spending her days and made a few minor adjustments. With the reevaluation came the desired change.

Each day when her children walked through the door, she focused all her attention and efforts on the kids. At three o'clock, Kathy put away whatever she was involved with and was ready to spend time with her children. As Kathy became more focused with family time, her home life improved. One of the first and most noticeable changes was the improvement in the children's grades. Kathy also found that the communication within the family improved. When they came home, Kathy discovered what happened at school that day. Because it was fresh on their minds, the kids gave Kathy immediate feedback. This helped Kathy understand where they struggled and why. *While focusing the majority of her attention on her kids, Kathy was able to clearly see their individual strengths and talents.*

Kathy helped her son discover he had a musical gift with the guitar. Not only did her efforts result in an improved relationship with her son, it bred other positive results. His newfound talent bred self-confidence and a positive group of friends who shared his passion for music. Kathy was able to seriously improve the happiness of her son. In doing so, Kathy discovered more powerful emotions than she had felt in the service of her neighbors.

In the other corner sat her daughter—a trickier project. Kathy had noticed a recent inclination in her daughter to wear clothing that Kathy felt was inappropriate for a girl her age. Resolved to help out as a servant to her own children, Kathy went to work delicately. Instead of sending her daughter to the mall with money to buy new clothes, Kathy took the time to go with her. She would be there to watch the purchases made and perhaps understand these new and unique styles. As an added bonus, her daughter purchased clothes that she would wear in front of her mother (not foolproof, but a start). Their relationship improved greatly, most likely as a result of the time spent together rather than the clothes actually purchased. Also, now Mom had suggestions as to what looked "cute" when her daughter was getting ready for the day. Not only could she see that her daughter was happier with their new relationship, but the clothing did eventually begin to fit better and cover more skin.

With each small change Kathy made, her family life improved. Her Safe

Haven is functioning. While Kathy doesn't claim to have a perfect home, she is thrilled with the changes. She is the first to admit that the changes were not as difficult to implement as she thought they would be. More importantly, the changes were well worth her effort.

Protecting Your Most Important Clients— Example 2

Tracy, a single mom with two daughters, came up with a unique way of creating her Safe Haven. She was a good mom, but was having trouble showing affection to her girls. In return, her daughters were distant, never displaying much emotion to their mother. Worried because of her oldest daughter's new boyfriend, Tracy knew something needed to change. It was not that he was even that bad of a guy. This boy was just showering Tracy's daughter with a little too much inappropriate affection.

Tracy wanted to improve the situation in her home. She was nervous with the concept of expressing her love daily to her girls, so she decided to try something new. Here is Tracy's story:

> I began to think of my home as a day spa. My main job as
> the director was to empower and enable. I looked at my
> children as clients—clients I wanted to keep. With this
> small change in my attitude toward my daughters, our
> relationships improved immediately. A little pampering
> went a long way. I changed how I would approach touchy
> subjects. Instead of nagging them to get their homework
> done, I sat down with them individually and offered my
> help just as I would respectfully do for a client. It was hard
> for me to do at first. I found it worked best if I calmed
> myself before I began to work with them. After a busy
> day at the office, I had to take long, deep breaths to slow
> my system down. Once I was calm, I would sit close and

occasionally put my arm around them. I found when I sat calmly and waited for them to ask questions, we had some in-depth discussions. As our relationships grew stronger, my girls felt comfortable enough to confide in me.

With each small success, I was ready for the next step. At first, I was not sure exactly how I would express my love to my kids on a daily basis. I am not an emotional person, and showing affection is difficult for me. I was uncomfortable with how to go about saying it. I didn't want to overdo it or sound phony. One of my daughters is seven and the other fifteen. My first attempts were awkward. But with each try, I improved. I decided to tell them how grateful I was that they were born into our family. I was pleasantly surprised with both responses. My seven-year-old laughed and said, "Yeah, I guess it is a good thing I was born here. It's better that I came here than somewhere else like Australia." This gave me the confidence to approach my fifteen-year-old. I was sure my teenager would look at me strangely and wonder what I was up to. Instead, she smiled, gave me a quick hug, and said, "Thanks Mom, sometimes I forget."

The light that shone in both of their eyes made me realize how much they needed me to praise them. This one small act created a different feeling in our home . . . a warmth. I was so thrilled with their responses; it became fun trying to figure out new ways to tell them how much I cared for them. I began putting notes of appreciation in their lunches and praising them in front of their friends. I cannot definitely say if this new showing of affection had anything to do with it, but my teenager soon got rid of the overly affectionate boyfriend.

While Tracy's specific example is probably unique (especially to those who do not manage day spas), the principle is not. She found a way to direct attention at her most important clients—her children. In our own ways, most of us save our energy to be kind and courteous to those we interact with outside of our families. Without devaluing the importance of always being a good person, I suggest that we reevaluate those efforts and save our most valuable time and energy for those who matter most to us—our offspring. Tracy had to step out of her comfort zone to create her Safe Haven, but the positive responses from her girls helped Tracy continue with the change.

Spreading Yourself Too Thin—Example 3

David and Susan both worked full-time. With three small children, they found it difficult to accomplish all their tasks. Every day consisted of a long workday capped with a murderous commute. That is where it stopped for most of their colleagues. But as parents, David and Susan were not able to breathe after their commutes—they whisked themselves into a list of activities for the kids. Tuesday it was soccer, Wednesday piano and dance, Thursday a performing group at school, and so on through the weekend. David and Susan were committed to providing "normal" childhoods for their children by allowing them to pursue their interests. After all their activities were accomplished, their bodies needed nourishment—so it was on to preparing a meal, a couple loads of laundry, and a little light cleaning. Of course, homework was sandwiched somewhere in between. Twenty-four-hour markets were designed for families like David and Susan's. Susan had to do all her shopping after they put the kids to bed.

Living such a lifestyle did not permit them to simply enjoy life together as a family. They worked so hard to fulfill "responsibilities" that leisure activities were becoming less and less of an option. David and Susan were increasingly stressed. With the growing pressures came growing tension in the house. Yelling and contention were almost commonplace and faded only with the onslaught of another list of "duties" hanging over their heads. Susan hollered at the girls when their rooms were a mess. David worked long hours and seemed to always be tired and grumpy when he arrived home. He and Susan fought about David not helping out around the house. Fighting seemed to be the only form of communication they had. Things had to happen quickly at this lifestyle's pace, and yelling seemed to be the best way to get that done. The kids were not happy, and their behavior at school was getting out of control. Susan and David both knew something had to change. They decided to slow things down a bit.

Susan's income was greater than David's. Thus, it quickly became apparent that the only solution was for Susan to keep working full-time, and for David to cut back to part-time. Although the solution did not seem ideal in theory, such a creative approach seemed to be the answer. The decision gave David the opportunity to start a business venture he had investigated years ago. Also, such an arrangement proved to keep David much happier. His previous job had been stressful and created unneeded pressure. *He found he liked spending more time with the kids.* David and Susan decided with the children to cut back to one after school activity per child David also had time to take care of many of the household chores that stressed Susan. This, in turn, kept Susan happy and improved their relationship. David and Susan fought less. The noise and frustration inside the household was at a new, pleasantly low, level. The children began to notice the change in their parents. With the friction between their parents no longer present, the children did not seem to argue as much. They found no need to yell in response when no one was yelling at them.

Let us not assume that such changes in lifestyle came without sacrifices. David was unable to buy the boat he had his eye (and heart) set upon, and Susan survived with a worn-out kitchen longer than she had planned, but they both agreed that the minor adjustments they had made were working. With their Safe Haven intact, their home life drastically improved.

Like most of us, all three of these families had problems in their homes. But with a few changes and a little creativity, the problems were not all that difficult to solve. Change itself can be the toughest part of creating a Safe Haven. Unfortunately, ignoring warning signs can be a very easy task, and when parents continue to ignore the problems, nothing changes. The problems will not simply dissipate and go away by your ignoring them. They will likely escalate and destroy the possibility of a happy family life. The good news is that the solutions are really not that complicated. The most important element is a parent's ability to *recognize* and *admit* something is wrong. The second most important element is the *willingness* to make changes.

You may be frustrated with so much emphasis upon the parent as the one who needs to make changes. Unfortunately, there is no other way to rephrase the truth. To soften the truth, try shedding new light on the situation. Through humor, the greatest truths can become apparent and oftentimes a little more surmountable. To help us cope with those people who are forcing us to change, laughter bridges an otherwise uncomfortable and awkward gap. Here goes . . . How many psychiatrists does it take to change a light bulb? Only one, but the light bulb really has to want to be changed.

With most board games, rolling the dice and prancing around the board can only be so effective. At some point, the player needs to actively involve him- or herself in action activities (i.e., buying properties, climbing ladders, or eliminating other players). Thus we turn our focus briefly to action items that will help in the process of substantial changes.

Changes will not take place with your parenting skills or in your home unless you initiate them. Let's get started making a few changes:

1. Analyzing is a two-step process: macro-analysis and micro-analysis. First, analyze what the aura is in your home. Is it tense most of the time? Does everyone feel stressed trying to accomplish what needs to be done? Is there yelling and fighting? Don't try to fix anything just yet; merely make the assessment. Then closely analyze specific situations. Can you figure out what is causing

the tension? Your ability to analyze the situation properly may take time, which takes us directly to the second action item.

2. Be patient with yourself and with your children. Right now, your main goal is to keep a calm demeanor and pay attention. Adjustment takes time, but remember to be relentless in your search for a Safe Haven. The key is you. If you change how you react in tense situations, the entire attitude in your home will magically adapt. Although patience is listed as a second step between analyzing and acting, in reality, it must be exercised consistently throughout the process.

3. Act instead of react. Contention escalates when we react to problems. This will require change because reaction to a problem is what we do naturally. We instinctly act on first impressions that are based on unknown facts instead of trying to understand what is causing the problem. When problems arise, stop and try to figure out what the problem is, why it is happening, and what you can do to solve it. Understanding and analyzing the problem takes far more time and effort than having a minor explosion. Overreacting happens quickly and without any forethought. If you add enough anger to the situation, you may gain a false sense of power or assume (incorrectly) that you are in control. On the other hand, when we take the time to proactively resolve a situation, we take back control of ourselves and the situation. We are able to harness energy in a common direction leading to the establishment of our Safe Haven.

When you overreact, you are not in control; rather, you are completely out of control. *When you use anger, the ability to influence your child is lost.* I am not suggesting that you dilute the message you send. If you need to send a strong message, do it with forethought and understanding of how your child will react. Sending a strong message while in control of oneself is much more powerful and progressive than firing off first reactions to a misunderstood situation. This goes without mentioning the possible detriments of such outbursts. Keep your calm, sympathize with your child, and analyze the problem. I can guarantee your solutions will become more effective, and you will not damage your kids in the process. It is tough to implement this procedure, but with practice, you will get better at it.

Let me further illustrate this point with two more examples.

To Act or Be Acted Upon—Example 4

Trisha was nineteen and had struggled as a driver since she received her license at age sixteen. She had been in more "fender benders" than her father cared to admit. Despite her driving record, Trisha was a responsible girl. Working toward and paying for her college degree, Trisha had recently applied for a masters program. It is not as if she lacked direction. However, Trisha's dad had obvious reservations with the rising costs of his car insurance. The last accident had caused him, in anger, to threaten Trisha. With one more accident, she would have to buy her own car and pay for her own insurance. To most parents, that probably sounds like a fair decision. But analyzing the situation may prove different. Let's review what Trisha's father had done.

Trisha understood the penalty. She did not want to be involved in another car accident. Unfortunately, the inevitable came, and it happened again. On a snowy morning, Trisha had an early class and could not avoid the collision. The car in front of her stopped quickly and Trisha, along with her father's previously dented Toyota, slid into the back of a new Lexus. Trisha was terrified to face her father because she knew what was about to happen. No amount of tears or explanations about the slick roads could calm her father down. Trisha's father laid down the law. He told himself he needed to be in control of the situation, and through such control, he was to teach his child a lesson. The car privileges were revoked.

Trisha did not know what to do. With the money she made as a part-time waitress, she could not afford to buy a car along with the insurance. For Trisha, a car was a necessity to get to work and school. Trisha analyzed her situation and decided her only option was to drop out of school for a while to earn enough money to pay for the car. The timing would set her back a year in graduate school. She was crushed and angry . . . angry at herself, but infuriated with her dad.

As we analyze this example, I want you to ask yourself, was this the only possible solution? Most of us believe that effective parenting is setting stick rules and following through with the punishments.. With this belief system, it is easy to justify our actions. How else would Trisha become responsible? At some point in her life, Trisha must be accountable for the mishaps with her father's car. How many times must we be reminded that kids today need firm discipline?

In this chapter, I don't want you to focus on discipline or belief systems. We will discuss those topics in later chapters. For now, I want you to keep in mind that we are trying to create a Safe Haven. It is important to go back and resolve what was really going on with Trisha.

Remember the importance of acting versus reacting to our children's behavior. Teenagers and cars will always be a tough situation for parents. There is no escaping it. When Trisha had her first car accident, her father did not handle it calmly. Getting angry made him feel as if he was solving the problem. It also made him think he was in control of the situation. However, the anger was clouding his solution to the problem. Dad needed to scrutinize what was really going on in this situation:

Why did this happen, and why did it keep happening? Was Trisha speeding?

Was she talking on her cell phone and not paying attention to the driver in front of her?

Were there friends in the car with her distracting her attention?

The solution is not that difficult—just very hidden. Remember, Trisha has proven to be a responsible girl in other aspects of her life. An assessment should have been made during Trisha's early accidents. Trisha's dad needed to get in the car with her and go driving. He could have quickly discovered that Trisha's problem was not one of distraction or speeding. It was one of judgment. Trisha was following too closely behind other cars. When the car in front stopped, her reflexes were not quick enough, and she did not have the time to react.

Simple problem, simple solution. Trisha's father needed to spend time with Trisha behind the wheel, a sort of driver's re-education. Anger and discipline were not going to help Trisha fix this problem. This type of problem could easily be solved without destroying the relationship between father and daughter. After multiple driving lessons with her dad, Trisha would have learned what she was doing wrong. Dad could have saved himself oodles of money in car insurance if he had only taken this first step back when Trisha was sixteen.

It might be interesting to note that dear old Dad drives in a similar fashion to Trisha, riding the tail of the car in front of him. He too slams on his brakes at the last possible moment. The difference is that Dad has the ability to react quickly and is much better at avoiding the collisions than Trisha. Could it be a learned behavior?

When a child makes a mistake, anger is not the correct reaction. Most of us react far too quickly, which only adds to the frustration in our homes and causes tension in our relationships. The key is to realize what you are doing and stop yourself before it happens. Ask yourself, "What could my child learn from this experience?"

As you continue reading (and with a little practice), this approach will become easier for you to implement. But for now, instead of reacting, just listen to your child and think through the situation. Analyze all possible solutions, and remember, when a child comes to you with a problem, he is not angry with you, just frustrated with a particular situation.

All of your child's fears and insecurities will be transposed to you. You are your child's dumping ground because you have created a safe place for your child to fall. Be thick-skinned. Search for what is truly troubling your child. Finally, *do not* take it personally.

The Trigger—Example 5

Paul walks in the door from school and drops his books on the floor—a big, loud sign he needs help and attention. His father, angry about the disturbance and also a little tense from a stressful day, confronts Paul with a loud voice, "What did you do that for?"

This gives Paul the excuse he needs to yell something back at his father. As the tension escalates, Paul's father then blows. He blames Paul for coming home in a bad mood and creating an unnecessary disturbance. Paul does not yet have the maturity to realize that he is the catalyst for the incident. He places blame on his father for responding so negatively to a few books being dropped.

This is an example of a very common occurrence that happens regularly in all of our homes. This brief incident shows how silly little conflicts can intrude in your Safe Haven. If you are trying to create and keep a positive environment in your home, be careful with every interaction. The saddest part of allowing anger to trigger from a situation like Paul's is that there is something hiding below the surface of his demeanor. Paul's actions are a subconscious plea for help with a different problem. He desperately needs to discuss something that is bothering him. If his parents do not seize this opportunity, it is quite possible no one else will and the situation will remain unsolved, ready to trigger another blast. It really does not matter who started the disagreement or who is to blame for the incident. When we react with anger, our precious moment as a teacher is lost.

Let's try again, keeping within the rules of our Safe Haven. Paul walks into the house after a long day at school. He slams his books loudly on the floor. (It may help to think of the books as a representation of his troubles.) This time Paul's father, instead of reacting to the situation, thinks to himself, *What could possibly be troubling Paul? What can I do to help?* Paul's father realizes that something is bothering him. The goal is to get Paul the help he needs. Paul's dad approaches Paul with a calm voice, putting his arm around his son's shoulders, and asks what he can do to help. He then lets Paul explain what has him upset. Paul's father does not pass judgment. He lets Paul talk as long as he needs to until the tension starts to leave. Paul's dad may ask questions that keep Paul expressing himself: "How did that make you feel?" or "I understand why you would be upset." When Paul is done talking, Paul's dad then reassures Paul that he understands.

The anger Paul is feeling will be diffused by the love Paul's father is extending.

As a parent, anytime you can get your child to verbalize what has gone wrong, the unpleasant behavior your child is exhibiting will change. The goal is to calm the child down so he or she can feel safety in the home. Achieving such a goal will create the environment necessary to discuss the problem. Sometimes all your children need to do is vent. Through talking, they will often come to their own solution to the problem.

Parents must provide calmness to bring down the level of frustration a child is feeling. Some parents do this through touch, possibly a hug. A gentle look on the face may be all that is needed, or even just a soft voice asking what is wrong. Whatever works best for your child is what you do. Caution: tears may start to flow. It may get them talking, or it may do nothing but calm them down a little so they don't feel so angry at the world. With this one small change in your reaction, your child enters a non-threatening environment. When they walk through the doors of your home, they should know that even though life outside may be hard on them, their home is a safe place.

The attitude you emit will affect them. In each one of these small incidents you encounter, you are giving your children tools that will help them return to the source of the frustration. Through example, you are preparing them for life as adults. You are showing them how to handle a tough situation.

The above example is fairly simple and easy to understand. The tough part is how a parent obtains and keeps this calm environment. After a stressful day, how do you change gears and calmly focus on your family? One might as well ask, "How do you eat an elephant?" The answer: one bite at a time. Take this process one step at a time. It takes patience, it takes practice, and it takes time. However, it is possible to live life this positively. Keep in mind that the people who understand this concept and are living it are having great success with their kids.

Creating a Safe Haven can be summed up in one word: sacrifice. It takes sacrifice on your part to make this work—a sacrifice that will pay off in the end. The word sacrifice sounds noble. It is noble, but the beauty of this particular sacrifice is that *you*, the parent, eventually reap the rewards if you make this Safe Haven a reality. Rewards will come in a variety of ways, some less apparent than others. Maybe it will help you avoid paying for counseling or drug rehabilitation, but the greatest reward you will ever possess is the satisfaction of watching your children lead successful, happy lives. No success tastes sweeter.

Alternatively, you can refuse to change your behavior and continue blaming your children for the atmosphere in your home. If this is your attitude, nothing in your household will ever improve. You will watch as the adolescent behavior your children exhibit as teenagers continues well into adulthood. Too many children are left to figure things out on their own during the teen years. If they do not get help, they will forever be stuck in a rut. After all, how many times have you met a twenty-nine-year-old that you thought was in his or her late teens?

Being judged as an adult when not an adult is not fair for a child. This is the time when children and teenagers should be learning skills for the rest of their lives, not being tested on materials unfamiliar to them. It is also the time for parents to be teaching these skills to their children. If you do not take the time to do it now, I guarantee you will pay for it later.

Troubleshooting the Safe Haven

As I teach the Safe Haven concept to parents, I am amazed at how most parents agree with the idea of the Safe Haven but struggle with changing their lifestyle so they may achieve it. To make the Safe Haven a reality, parents, you must change. In my parenting workshops, I noticed three common transformations that need to be made: learn how to de-stress your life, get rid of the tough love, and relax and enjoy your children.

De-Stress

Let's go back to our first bite of that elephant: how to stay calm. The first thing you must do is de-stress your life. Begin by analyzing your days: Are you working every day and then coming home to a mountain load of laundry, a dirty house, and a family hungry for dinner? Could you work fewer hours? Find a more satisfying job? This piece of the puzzle is totally up to you.

To be an effective parent, you must have a clear head to calmly solve problems. So this first bite is the one where you take control of your own life. It should not control you. You, and only you, can figure out what needs to be sacrificed. Decide what is most important in your life and what you can do without. This might mean canceling a business meeting, getting off the phone, or finding a new job. No halfhearted efforts will work here. You need to believe in this and be willing to make changes. Give this step some deep thought. Be creative, and consider all possibilities. The decisions you make here will come from within. Realize the power you have in your home is yours. Nothing will change unless you do!

You may not have to give up anything at all. In fact, it might be that you need to add something to your daily routine. Figure out what you must do to be calm and peaceful. Is it exercise? Do you need to uplift yourself with a good book or socialize with new friends? Figure out what it is you need and then ask for help from a friend, a church group, a coworker, or your spouse. Sometimes we try to be so self-sufficient that we are exhausted by the time we get to our kids. When we shortchange ourselves, we end up hurting the ones we love most. So figure out what it takes to get that peacefulness within yourself, and ask for help.

Many of us find this concept easy to understand but difficult to implement. There are enough self-help books written on this topic to let us know that people in every stage of life struggle with finding what it is that makes them happy. I promise you that it is possible to find this calm within yourself. Your home life will vastly improve once you take care of it. To create the Safe Haven, finding peace within yourself is an important change you must take the time to make.

Tough Love

You may understand the concepts of the Safe Haven but feel uncomfortable administering them because it appears as if you are going too easy on your child. Many adults feel that to raise responsible children, tough discipline needs to be imposed. I've often heard this referred to as "tough love."

Many professionals claim that a lack of strict discipline is the problem with today's kids. This is simply not true. In fact, just the opposite is true. If your home environment involves overly strict parents with rigid discipline, your kids will at some point rebel, publicly or privately.

Tough love is a lazy parenting technique that exhibits itself when a parent is tired or not willing to put in the effort to figure out what they need to do to help a child. From personal experience with my own children, when I got tough, they quit trying. Children do not need toughness. They need love, understanding, and help.

It is important to remember when working with kids that if something is not working, there is an alternate solution, so try something new. Do not keep dishing out the same punishment again and again. When you dole out threats and in return all you get is the same response, change is needed—change from you, not your child. If your child makes a mistake and you revert back to a tough love technique, try asking yourself the famous Dr. Phil question: "How is that working for you?" If you are truly honest with yourself, I think you will find you are not progressing with your child but instead destroying the relationship. In coming chapters, we will talk more in-depth about teaching correct principles and motivating. For now, while you are trying to effectively create the Safe Haven, give your child a hug and back off the tough love.

Relax, Enjoy Your Children, and Just Be

For a short time, forget all the rules you have set for your household. Don't worry about the lessons you feel you must teach your child. As you progress, you will learn new ways to effectively teach your children. The inability of parents to take the time to relax with their kids is a key warning sign of problems within the family. When parents find themselves struggling with this concept of leisure time, they launch the whole family down a slippery slope towards unhappiness.

For now, do not try to fix your child. Focus on having a good time together. Sometimes we forget to just be. Many of us have simply forgotten how to play. Play with your children. Roll with them in the grass, tickle them, play games. To have happy children, you must play with them. *Our children learn more from our examples than from our efforts to improve upon them.* Teaching by example should make us realize where we need to put our emphasis. If we want to improve our children, we need to improve ourselves. It may sound too simple, but the parents who enjoy spending time with their children are also the ones who are having the most success in their parenting.

Resources

Are you still stuck, unable to create a Safe Haven? If you are struggling with this concept, I have a few reading suggestions.

First, a book by C. Terry Warner, *Bonds That Make Us Free*. This book is particularly helpful if you are trapped in negative emotions. Life is so much richer if you can free yourself of negative emotions. By addressing the root causes of our emotions, it is easier to make changes from within. In his book, Warner teaches how to have a change of heart. He can help you understand how to bond as a family. Sometimes as parents we get stuck because we look upon our child as the enemy. Warner explains how to face your own fears— fears which get in the way of loving your children.

> We try to change the negative attitude, but cannot see how to make it work. When "stuck," we think the problem is with other people. It lies within us. We need a diagnosis. The truth is the cure. It is in the darkness of their eyes that men lose their way. As long as our hearts are wrong, we can't do right when our heart's not right.[6]

Mr. Warner challenges us to test everything. Try to quit demanding justice and ask yourself, *"Might I be in the wrong?"*

When working with children, it is important to do the right thing for the right reason. Children can spot a phony a mile away.

Warner continues, "By ceasing self-betrayal, we abandon our reasons for accusing others in our hearts. And when accusation ceases, we are able to see others as they really are and to love them."[6]

Another resource to help you make those needed changes is the book *Core Transformation* by Connirae and Tamara Andreas.[7] This book can help you do your best work as a parent. The Andreas sisters teach how to have a sense of acceptance, not judgment, which is very important when working with children. You need immediate help if you are screaming and yelling at your kids and see no way to adapt your behavior. It is possible to change the way you react to things. The wisdom you will gain from this book will help you discover your core state and how to transform each intended outcome.

Checklist

How you approach your child will make all the difference in how effective you will be within your Safe Haven. Using the proper techniques can diffuse a potential disastrous encounter.

1. Delay your responses. Postpone actions or a reply until you have thought about what just happened or what was said. Respond at a later, calmer time. This makes it possible to act instead of react.

2. Discover your hot buttons. These buttons are the first sign to let you know the situation is about to spin out of control. When you feel yourself welling up with anger, remove yourself from the conflict. Pay attention each time this happens, and consider ways you can change the results before the next conflict.

3. Have reverence for your child.

4. Use humor. We all make mistakes daily. If you can see humor in a situation, it will be easier to calmly find a solution.

5. Be tolerant of differences. Problems are inevitable. Get thick-skinned about the differences. Each person in a family should be allowed his or her own point of view, regardless of age.

6. Allow for slothfulness. Each child (and parent) will need his own personal down time. Lying around watching Saturday morning cartoons or sleeping in can qualify as "normal" behavior. Don't get angry, try to coax, or cajole. Give your child a break. You may even consider joining in.

7. Choose your words carefully. Remember, angry words will deeply wound a child. In his book *Ageless Body, Timeless Mind*, Deepak Chopra states:

> [T]he language we use to refer to ourselves is of tremendous importance. Child psychologists have found that young children are much more deeply influenced by ascriptive statements from their parents (e.g., "You're a bad boy"; "You're a liar"; "You're not as smart as your sister") than by prescriptive statements (e.g., "Always wash your hands before eating"; "Don't put your toys in your mouth"; "Be on time for school"). In other words, telling a child *what he is* makes a much deeper impression that telling him *what to do*. The mind-body stem actually organizes itself around such verbal experiences, and the wounds delivered in words can create far more permanent effects than physical trauma, for we literally create ourselves out of words.[8]

8. Play with your children.

The information in this chapter is important because the Safe Haven is your foundation. If you find yourself floundering, it will help to return to this chapter and continually review the principles of the Safe Haven. Your creation of the Safe Haven will instill confidence in your child that the world is a friendly place.

Instinctual Mandates

We are born with instinctual mandates, things we do instantly without thought or decision. As adults, we have lost most of our spontaneity. We have learned to suppress our natural reaction toward life. Children fortunately still have it. Young children continually express their aliveness. They dance using every part of their body, spin until they fall down, yell at the top of their lungs. Nothing inhibits them, and everything interests them. Children are the epitome of happiness. Life really doesn't get better than this.

As they grow and develop, things change: a sibling joins the family, they struggle at school, playmates make fun of them. They become self-conscious, fear sets in, and they slowly lose their sense of being fully alive. In one form or another, this happens to all of us.

So, as adults, what do we do? We search for this sense of fulfillment in other ways. We dress fancy, buy big houses, and drive expensive cars, all in the name of success the American way. It is crazy, but what we are really looking for in life is that aliveness we once felt. We have acquired fears and lost a sense of what really matters in life. So we run, take exotic vacations, drink, take drugs, or dream our way through movies. The problem lies in living in a world and in relationships that do not bring us happiness. We act defensively, have feelings of inadequacy, and feel threatened. I believe if we could stop feeling fear, lose our defensive behaviors and inadequate feelings, and get back to what really matters in life (our relationships), we could feel the aliveness again.

Living in a Safe Haven will not only give your child a sense of safety, but everyone in your household will benefit. You know how a smile or a kind word can change your day. Imagine how safe and confident your children will feel every day when they leave your home and return knowing they are loved and accepted.

You are the one who does this affirming for your child. Unfortunately, your children will have plenty of disapproving people in their lives. Don't put your name on that list. You have much to offer your child. There is no one else who knows and understands your child like you do. No one can encourage your child or protect your child like you can. The support, protection, and love you give your child are far more important than the discipline. Your children should feel the spirit of love, respect, and safety when they are near you. When they are around you, your children will be blessed from your wisdom and good judgment. Love your children.

As we continue forward, keep this in mind: the basic unit of society is the family. Society will eventually fail without its basic unit. Currently, the family is under attack. It is our responsibility as parents to protect that sacred family unit. The power and influence that a parent has to offer is incredible. If you take your role seriously, if you govern your dominion wisely, and if you honor and protect your family, happiness and success will come.

Get started creating your Safe Haven. Do it now!

CHAPTER TWO

Building Relationships

Once you understand the components of the Safe Haven, expand and move forward with the next important step: understanding your relationship. If you have been successful with your quest to build a Safe Haven, you will notice that you are already on the path toward a better relationship with your kids. But don't stop creating; there is more you can do.

Bonds of friendship and loyalty are links in a chain that will forever bond you and your child. *When your child is confronted with critical decisions, the strength of your relationship will make the difference in your child's ability to resolve them.*

Improving the parent/child relationship begins just as the Safe Haven did: analyze the relationship between you and your child. Ask yourself, "What is my relationship with my kids?" "Do we enjoy spending time together?" "Do we have plenty of things to talk about?" "Are we able to relax together one-on-one?" "Do we share any common interests?"

For some parents, the ability to scrutinize the relationship will come naturally. To others, it can be a very difficult thing to do. This process will vary from child to child. With one child, it may be simple. You understand each other and get along beautifully. Yet, with another child, there are few common interests, so it may be difficult to enjoy spending time together.

Problems similar to this occur in all families. This struggle can occur between mother and son, father and daughter, mother and daughter, or father and son. We all have unique personalities and prefer certain behaviors. It is important to acknowledge the fact that these differences exist, but this realization does not let you off the hook. It is the first step toward change. As a parent, it is your duty to build the relationship. Your child needs to know that you love and accept him or her for who he or she is. There are a variety of creative ways you can learn to work through the problems that exist between individuals.

As you begin to assess your situation, take note of what is going on when you are with your child. This exercise is designed to show you how your child perceives you, not for you to understand your child. Be aware of every interaction and conversation you have with your child. Instead of focusing on what your child says to you, for this particular assessment pay close attention to your responses. Write down every conversation that occurs, even the ones that are about minor, day-to-day issues. As you jot things down, notice what your conversations are about, then analyze this data. Patterns will begin to emerge:

- Are you spending any time discussing topics that interest your child?
- Do your conversations flow freely?
- Do you ever sit down and watch a television program together?
- Is there any fun or laughter in your discussions?
- Are the tones of most chats positive or negative?

- Do you spend the majority of your conversations discussing tasks that need to be accomplished, or improvements that need to be made?

This is usually an eye-opening exercise. Throughout the process, you will surprise yourself with the results. This exercise is designed to help you understand the type of relationship you have with your child and to determine how your child feels about you. It should also give you an accurate idea of why your children are responding in certain ways to your requests or comments. If the conversations you are initiating consist mostly of negativity, the responses you get from your child will also be negative.

You may even discover that most interactions with your child are good, and there are only a few topics with which you struggle. Once you can identify those issues, you will be able to change the way you approach your child. The process of correcting a few issues here and there is easy. The difficulties arise when you cannot identify the problem.

If you find there is continual conflict between you and your children and they rarely respond positively to you, pay close attention to how you talk to them and the content of your conversations. *Your children will not want to interact with you if they know that every conversation they have with you will be something they do not want to hear.*

To build a strong relationship with your child, you need to strive for more pleasant interactions. If the majority of past conversations include lists of things they need to do, ways they can improve themselves, or other items of business that your children view as unpleasant, they will avoid any dialogue with you, they will shun spending time together, and, even worse, they may begin to shut you out completely.

Kids do need responsibility, but no one wants to be nagged. If that is how you are perceived by your child, something needs to change. There is a better way. In later chapters, we will discuss how to create a more responsible child. The main focus for this chapter is building the relationship. Before it becomes possible to have a child who accepts responsibility, a good relationship must exist. So be patient with the process. *Relationship first, responsibility later.*

Once you understand your relationship, you can build upon it. Find something you and your child have in common: a sport, music, or an interesting book. Sometimes this can be difficult. Between some parents and children, discovering a mutual interest may seem almost impossible.

If you cannot come up with anything, let me suggest an easy, no-fail solution: food. I have yet to meet a teenage boy who would turn down an offer to get something to eat. Just imagine the surprised look on your son's face when, out of the blue, you suggest taking him to his favorite fast-food restaurant for whatever his stomach desires. Use your trip as a chance to talk. During this time, do not allow yourself to criticize, remind, or assign. Your time interacting is brief, so don't blow it.

Be together and have fun. Remember, there can be no negatives coming from your mouth. No advice-giving, judgment calls, or improvements requested. Just spend relaxed time getting to know each other better as this is a time for you to get reacquainted. That is your only goal. Keep it simple, and don't expect too much. If your first few encounters do not go as well as planned, be patient. It may take numerous outings for your child to trust the new you. Your relationship will improve with time if you carry out such activities as often as possible.

Teenage girls like to eat, too. But a food offering may not mean as much to your daughter as a shopping trip might. Be creative and thoughtful in your proposals. Choose something simple that you know is important to your child. You will know when you are on the right track if your child actually agrees to accompany you and allows the two of you to be seen together in public places.

Most parents find this project easy to do with younger children. If you begin these fun excursions while your kids are young, you are on the right path to building strong relationships. It becomes more of a challenge during the teen years. When it comes to dealing with teenagers, you need to make it a priority to spend time together on a regular basis. If your relationship has eroded to a very low level, teenagers can make this process difficult. They may refuse to talk or, even worse, say only the things they know will offend their parents.

Stay pleasant, be thick-skinned, and do not let it get to you.

If the parent/child relationship is not good, it will be tough to rebuild. But remember that your child is challenging you. Stay strong and dedicated, and always show love. You are the adult here. As their parent, you have the ability to do this. Your children really do want you around, and more importantly, they need you around. This process, like the Safe Haven, takes time, patience and a little creativity.

How to Skateboard Without the Baggy Pants

Let's try a sample scenario: what if your child loves skateboarding, and that is all he wants to do? Surprisingly enough, this particular activity is what you detest most about the way your child spends his free time. Skateboarding may be a hard subject for you to tackle, but because he loves it, skateboarding will be the easiest topic to get him talking. You just have to figure out how.

Try this: First, rent a video on aggressive skating. I think you will be surprised how enjoyable this activity might be. Have you ever watched aggressive skaters? While one of my kids was home from school for weeks with a broken leg, I had this opportunity. They are pretty wild. These kids do incredible things. You may not be thrilled with the low riding jeans or the long hair, but remember, you are not passing judgment. You are not trying to teach your child anything. You are just watching this for entertainment . . . and to build a relationship with your child. Put away fears that your child will be a failure if he loves this sport. Relax and enjoy yourself. If you can build a good relationship with your child, he will eventually emulate your values, not those of the skateboarders.

After you watch the video, you now have something to talk about. Keep it positive because you must believe in your child and the relationship. To get the conversation rolling, ask your child to explain how they do those stunts or what kind of skateboards they ride and why. If you take the time to show interest without being critical, I guarantee you will get a response from your child and the beginning of an interesting conversation. The key is no criticism and no judgment.

You are not allowed to mention to your child that there is not a future in skateboarding. Do not hit him with the reality that only one kid out of a zillion is ever awarded a sponsorship or that it is impossible to make money at this sport. As adults, we know that these statements are probably true, but they will only be perceived as negative and will discourage your child. Your child will eventually figure this out without your help. Growing up is hard to do, so let him keep his imagination and be a child while he still can. Your job is to support your kids, not crush their dreams. *If you speak negatively about the things your children are interested in, you will be the one they resent.*

Support them, be involved, and let them go as far as they can with a dream. Then reality will take its course. When there is no future in something, your children will move on. Have faith in them, and concentrate on building the relationship.

As you try this, you may become tied up in knots, trying desperately to say the right thing. Here are a few ideas from Spencer Johnson, author of *The One-Minute Father*. Mr. Johnson gives us simple techniques to help our children discover positive aspects of their personalities. He calls his method "One-Minute Praising."

1. I tell my children ahead of time that I am going to praise them when they do something that makes me feel good. And I encourage them to do the same with me.

2. I catch my children doing something right.

3. I tell my children specifically what they did.

4. Then I tell them how good I feel about what they did and why it makes me feel so good.

5. I stop talking for a few seconds. The silence lets them feel the good feeling themselves.

6. Then I tell them that I love them.

7. I end the praising with a hug, or at least a light touch to let them know I care.

8. The praising is short and sweet. When it's over, it's over.

9. I realize that it takes me only a minute to praise my children. But feeling good about themselves may last them for a lifetime.

10. I know that what I am doing is good for my children and for me. I feel really good about myself.[1]

In every interaction you have with your children, try to remember three simple goals: love, guide, and protect. It is necessary when building a relationship to understand all three.

Love

Do you remember when your child was an infant and everything she did was incredible? It was an exciting moment when she lifted her head, spoke her first word, or began crawling. If you have forgotten, watch the parent of a new baby. That look of adoration is an incredible thing to witness.

Now compare that look with the looks often exhibited by the parents of teenagers. Often, instead of adoration, teens receive looks of mistrust, apprehension, disgust, and mostly fear from their parents. Try to remember that although teenagers have adult bodies, they are still children. Teenagers need that adoration and love. If they are typical teens, they do not realize how difficult they can make it for a parent to show this love. As their parent, you can never give up showing love to your child.

Guide

Most guidance comes in the form of examples. As parents, we feel we have to tell our kids everything, and often we are too free with the advice. We usually find ourselves handing out so much advice that our kids quit paying attention. Listening is far more important. If you truly listen to your child, you will begin to understand more about this child and the ways you can help him.

Pay attention to your children, especially while they are young. You can learn so much. Watch what interests them, and observe how they do things. This will help you guide them now and later in life. As you try to build or rebuild your relationship with your child, listen and learn. If you do this with gentleness and love, soon your son or daughter will begin asking you for advice and guidance.

Protect

Keep your children safe, not only from physical harm, but also guard their emotional well-being. Never let a spouse, teacher, coach, or any other adult say or do anything that would harm your children emotionally. You have the power to control who you let into your child's life, so protect it.

These three goals will be discussed throughout the book. As you continue reading, you will discover how important they really are. This relationship you are forming between parent and child is the most important relationship in his or her life. Guard it.

CHAPTER THREE

Understanding
Ideals

Parenthood. All of us arrive at this challenging responsibility with a variety of backgrounds, experiences, and reasons for becoming a parent. Before having children, we tucked away, somewhere in the back of our minds, an idealized version of how our lives would be. Many of us envisioned our children before they were born . . . what they would look like, how they would behave, and how they would not behave. These ideals were most likely created from the memories of our own childhood or from observations we made while watching other families.

I pictured my children as clean, neatly dressed, and very well-behaved, not at all the disgusting, snot-nosed kids I had witnessed "acting out" at movie theaters or restaurants. At that time, I remember thinking, *How irresponsible could the parents of those children be, letting their kids behave like animals?* When we form most of our ideals, we have no idea what we are in for when we have children. Nor do we think we will ever be asking ourselves, "What have I done wrong? Where did those perfect children I once dreamed of disappear to?"

Your picture may vary or even be a little more realistic than most, but each of our dreams reflects what is, or is not, acceptable in our own eyes. Every parent has hopes, dreams, and goals for his or her family. Dreams and goals are good things, but what happens when these dreams meet reality? We want our families to match the mental image we have created. Often, when things don't work out, disappointment is a natural reaction. As a parent, it is difficult to accept when your children do not meet the standards you have set for them.

As adults, most of us have had our fair share of experience with disappointments. The healthiest way to handle disappointment is to learn what you can from the situation and move forward. Although no one likes to admit it, disappointment can be a positive thing. However, these disappointments will become problems if we become discouraged and refuse to move ahead—especially if our feelings of disillusionment are so strong they negatively affect our children.

Children know when their parents are disappointed in them. They may not totally understand what they are feeling and why, but they do know when they have let their parents down. The emotions we transfer to our kids, verbal or non-verbal, affect how they feel about themselves. Children internalize. They blame themselves. Even teenagers have yet to gain the maturity to surmise that the disappointment they are feeling from their parent belongs with the unrealistic dreams of the parent—not with the child.

Our dreams must match our eyes. That statement is important because most ideals are just that—ideal. Dreams almost never turn out exactly as we have planned. It reminds me of going into a movie theater for an afternoon matinee. It is such a relaxing way to spend the afternoon. All troubles are forgotten, and you can focus on the narrative portrayed on the big screen.

The show eventually ends, you walk outside into the bright sunlight, and immediately you are shocked back into reality. All the stresses and problems of the day have returned. Unlike the movies, none of our lives have fairy tale endings. Life is real. Your kids are real.

The more realistic methods you use to parent, the greater your success will be. Let me use Cheryl as an example. Cheryl talks about the dreams she envisioned for her daughter.

Breeding a Superstar

When Cheryl was pregnant with her daughter, she loved the sport of tennis. She played every day until her eighth month of pregnancy, when she was too large to compete. Thank goodness Wimbledon was on television. Even though she was unable to play tennis, she could watch it on TV.

This was years ago when Chris Evert was at the top of her game. As Cheryl watched Chris play, she reflected upon her life and wondered why, when she was younger, she didn't push herself to be more competitive? She felt a little sad that her time had come and gone.

She decided then and there she would give the child she was carrying the chance she had let pass her by. She could provide her daughter with the opportunities that she'd needed years ago. If she started when she was young, Cheryl thought her daughter could be a top contender in tennis. It was exciting for Cheryl just to think about what her daughter could do with her life, all she could be, with Cheryl's plans and her dedication.

For fifteen years, Cheryl stuck with her goal. She enrolled her daughter in tennis lessons as soon as she could walk and hold a racquet. She played a lot of tennis as a young girl. And she was good.

Cheryl's plan worked brilliantly until her daughter's teenage years. She no longer wanted to dedicate her life to one sport. She liked soccer and track. At first, this was fine with Cheryl, as long as the other sports didn't interfere with tennis. Her daughter's closest friends did not play tennis, and she often chose to hang out with them instead of practicing. It bothered Cheryl when she did this. She felt her daughter was wasting precious time.

Couldn't she find new friends, friends that would keep her involved in tennis? Cheryl coerced, pleaded, and tricked her daughter into matches.

It soon became obvious that her idea of what she wanted in life did not match Cheryl's plan. There were many arguments, discussions, and screaming matches about tennis. Cheryl's husband eventually stepped between them and helped Cheryl realize that it was her daughter's life to live and not Cheryl's. Cheryl's daughter had her own plans. Her mother had to step back and let her live her life. It was a tough adjustment.

Now, as Cheryl looks back, she realizes it took her husband and his wisdom to help her realize that she was slowly destroying her relationship with her daughter over tennis. It was Cheryl's dream, not her daughter's. Once she could clearly see the damage she was doing, Cheryl was embarrassed to realize that she'd had her daughter's life planned before she was even born.

Cheryl had set unrealistic goals for her daughter. She had imposed her own dreams into her daughter's life, dreams that her daughter was not comfortable with. It is important to help your child attain a goal, but it has to be her goal, not yours.

What Cheryl was trying to do is very common. Many children don't have a clue what dreams they want to pursue, so parents step in with ideas. There is nothing wrong with helping your child find a passion. Offer suggestions and support, and then be available to assist your children as they discover the directions they want to head in. Be careful not to push too hard. Some kids will be comfortable picking one goal and sticking with it. Most children need to try a variety of activities. Your job is to provide the opportunities, all the while monitoring your own behavior. Their dreams cannot become your dreams, or vice versa.

Colin Young, who pitched in the Rockies and Red Sox organizations from 1999 to 2004, is a great example of incredible drive and motivation. How did Colin's parents motivate him to be so dedicated and successful?

Colin says they never pushed him.

> People often ask what my parents' role was in my climb to
> professional baseball. I tell those people that my parents
> were supportive of my love of baseball and gave me every
> opportunity to succeed. My father was a football coach
> and knew nothing of baseball, and my mother did not play
> sports in high school. Whether I played a great game or a
> terrible game, my parents always treated me with support
> and love. They never "pushed" me in any way, and any-
> thing that I accomplished was because of my own desires
> and their support. They had complete trust in my coaches,
> and I was very lucky to have great ones along the way. So
> when you look at your child and you see a major league
> baseball player or a professional football player, under-
> stand that they may think of themselves as something very,
> very different. It's not about you, and if it is, it's probably
> the reason your kid sucks. Parents: don't be the reason for
> your kid's failures. They're under enough pressure already.[1]

In his book, *Ageless Body, Timeless Mind*, Deepak Chopra M.D. stresses
letting go of expectations.

> The paradox is that to get the most passion from life, you
> must be able to stand back and be yourself. Finding your
> freedom is necessary, and it involves letting go of expec-
> tations, preconceived outcomes, and egotistical points of
> view. Consider two mothers, each standing in the aisle of a
> supermarket trying to handle an upset child who is crying
> loudly and attracting attention. One mother is angry and
> embarrassed. Her primary motive is to stop the child
> from making a scene, but of course this doesn't work with

small children. When they are upset, they are upset. Their feelings are their world, and making a scene in the market doesn't mean anything to them. So when the mother commands, "Alright, stop crying. I mean it, stop right now," the child knows that his feelings aren't really being heard and therefore he isn't being allowed to really exist. The mother just wants a result; she wants things to turn out a certain way.

The second mother, on the other hand, sees that her child is genuinely upset, and she doesn't care about how she looks to others. She isn't thinking about the situation as it affects her; instead, she feels for her child and wants him to be happy again. She says things such as, "What's wrong? Did something scare you? It's alright, I'm here." The words she uses are not the critical thing—she might just pick up and caress her child for a moment. The child's quantum mechanical body senses that his feelings have been understood.

Therefore, there is no threat, because his mother's intention is to heal, not merely to end a disagreeable situation.

Being oriented to your true self, not to your self-image, is the most basic healing attitude anyone can take. When you are oriented to the self, you use your feelings, your needs, and your values as a jumping-off point for finding that level of your being where feelings, needs, and values are already fulfilled.[2]

Does it really matter what others think of you as a parent? If the ideals you have set for yourself as a parent include impressing the neighbors, you will not find success with your children. Pay attention to your child and his or her needs. Get rid of any false pictures of how life should be, and concentrate on what it is. If you have problems understanding this concept, listen to your child. Children have an excellent understanding of their needs. To succeed, they cannot do it alone. They need your support.

This is another "easy to understand, but difficult to implement" concept. Parenting would be so much easier if life would go according to our plans. If our children would simply listen to us, we could make their lives successful. But that is not how it works. As parents we have to remember that the learning skills our children gain come through the process of living life, not from having lived it. Too often as parents we get caught up in the idea of producing a professional athlete or a world-renowned brain surgeon.

Kids are real. Listen closely to them, and you will understand that they have dreams and goals. If you don't see them for what they are, they will eventually make you see them clearly one way or another. Clear your head of ideals and do not set unrealistic goals. This child is not your possession, but a child who possesses unique gifts. Children are capable of making choices if you will let them.

As you make your ideals more realistic, watch closely for two destructive habits: blame and comparison. They are alive and thriving in our families.

Blame

Earlier we talked about parental disappointment when our children don't live up to our dreams. When our children don't fit images we have created, the most common reaction from the adults in their lives is to blame the child. "Why can't they be like this?" or "Why don't they do it this way?"

Many times as parents, if our kids don't behave how we think they should, we feel humiliated or embarrassed, so we inflict blame, which then creates a child full of guilt.

A sure sign you are failing is continual blame on the child. Blame is one of those damage-causers you want to stay far, far away from.

Why do we do this? Somehow, as parents, it makes us feel more in control if we can find one person to blame for what has happened. We like to have a scapegoat. Cheryl, for example, dumped the blame upon her daughter and her daughter's friends when the girl wanted to quit tennis. If she could blame someone or something, Cheryl could ignore the reality that her daughter did not have the desire to play tennis. This is a perfect example of the dreams-meeting-reality concept.

Unfortunately, blame usually works and is an excellent method to guilt your child into doing what you want him or her to do. However, I'll warn you: you will pay for using this form of manipulation on your child. It kills motivation and will slowly destroy any relationship you have built with your child. Using blame will take away the trust your child has in you.

Comparison

As stated earlier, many ideals come from observations made over the years. Problems arise when observing turns into comparing. It is tough to be realistic about your dreams when it appears everyone around you, like neighbors and friends, seem to have it all. Comparing your life to that of a neighbor is a ticket for failure.

Many of us have friends whose lives appear perfect. They lead ideal lives inside immaculate homes with flawlessly dressed children and husbands with perfect hair. It appears as if there is a never-ending supply of money. A surreal picture designed to make all the neighbors envious. I have witnessed this scenario enough times to know that the truth is rarely portrayed correctly.

Perfection is not possible. If necessary, say this to yourself again and again: no one is perfect. The family you are idealizing is not perfect. There are problems you don't see. It is only in your mind that they are perfect. Never judge your family according to the standards of another.

You cannot beat yourself up over not measuring up. Believing in perfectionism will make life too difficult for your spouse, your children, and yourself. Not only does your false image negatively affect you, but this behavior will transfer to your child. The last thing you want to do to your children is give them the impression that self-worth depends upon appearance.

Love yourself for who you are because perfectionism makes a person rigid and judgmental. Who wants to be around that? Relax! Have some fun. Accept your flaws and those of your children. You are an individual. Your child is an individual. Be what you are and rejoice in what you are. If you can do this, you will get more pleasure out of life and discover success and happiness along the way.

C.S. Lewis describes the false pride found in perfectionism:

> Pride gets no pleasure out of having something, only out of having more of it than the next man. We say that people are proud of being rich, or clever, or good-looking, but they are not. They are proud of being richer, or cleverer, or better-looking than others. If everyone else became equally rich, or clever, or good-looking there would be nothing to be proud about. It is the comparison that makes you proud: the pleasure of being above the rest. Once the element of competition has gone, pride has gone.[3]

It is possible to change and create a new dream of the ideal family. Start by evaluating your family as they truly are and be proud of each member. The life they have chosen may not be what you had imagined for them, but that is OK. Their happiness should be your ultimate goal.

Belief Systems

Your dreams must match reality. When the workings of your family are not progressing smoothly, you may have to double-check your belief system. To make an honest evaluation of your family, it is important to understand what a belief system is and how it came about. We often see the world not as it is, but as we are. Hyrum W. Smith discusses what he calls "Belief Windows" in his book *Pain Is Inevitable, Misery Is Optional*:

We all have a unique way of looking at the world. How we view something depends on many things: our religious beliefs, our life experiences, how we were raised, and our culture. Everything we have experienced determines how we view the world. I like the label Hyrum Smith gave it—belief windows.

> The Belief Window . . . [is an] invisible window [that]
> filters everything we see and experience, and our per-
> ceptions—so filtered—affect the decisions we make, the
> actions we take, and ultimately the results we get. [The]
> basic premise was that since our behavior is significantly
> influenced by what we believe to be true about ourselves
> and the world, behavior change could take place only
> when an "incorrect" belief on a person's window was
> replaced by a better belief, one more in line with reality.

Our beliefs affect our behavior. If our belief system is correct, the decisions and actions we make will meet our needs. Having your needs met is a good indicator that your beliefs will line up with things as they really are. If throughout your life you do not like the results you are getting, or they are painful or harmful, your belief windows might need some cleaning. This is not an easy process because the beliefs on our windows are what we perceive to be true.

To simplify how easily our belief windows are formed, let me give you a brief example. If, as a young child, you are taught that lemons are red, you will believe that a lemon is red in color. The truth is that lemons are yellow, but at that point, you only know what you have been taught. Until further knowledge is presented to you, the color yellow is red.

Let me give you another example. If you had a belief on your belief window that children should be seen and not heard, as a parent, you would have very little tolerance for a gregarious child, so your natural reaction would be one of strong discipline. Generally, when a child is parented with rigid discipline, the behavior results in some form of rebellion. Whatever form of rebellion the child chose—low grades, underage drinking, getting a tattoo—it would be something that negatively affects you, the parent. As you try to make sense of it all, you would probably believe you had made the correct decision; it was the child who was incorrect. Whatever you believe, you must admit you are not getting the response hoped for.

Let's adapt this scenario. If, as a parent, you notice you are not getting the results you expected and your child is refusing to respond to your discipline, you can do one of two things. (1) Continue with the strict discipline and get the same results, or (2) you could change your parenting practices and watch your child's behavior improve. Of course, every parent would choose the latter.

The difficulty with belief windows lies in the cleaning, or in other words, the change. Our acceptance of what is on our windows is the cause of most of our problems in life. The beliefs on our windows exert a powerful influence on our actions and behavior. No pain is more painful than that we inflict upon ourselves. If the results of your behavior are not meeting your needs, the problem is a belief on your belief window.

We often accept what is on our windows without question, which is the cause of most of our problems in life. This can sometimes spiral, causing situations like child abuse and alcoholism to continue generation through generation. If you are not happy, if your children are not doing well, you might be deceiving yourself. Ask yourself these very straightforward questions: Am I happy? Are my children happy? If not, why? Do not rationalize and pretend what you want to happen is actually happening in a situation. Be honest with yourself. If you feel confused, there are professionals, friends, families, and religious leaders we can ask for help. Continuing to live in a world of denial causes more pain. You must make sure that what you believe to be true is closely aligned with reality.

How do you change this self-deception? First, you must realize that we all have faulty beliefs on our windows. But the willingness to recognize the need to question and change your belief window is a sign of maturity. Personal growth is the process of challenging and updating what is on your belief window. Be open to change and growth.

Steve and Julie are perfect examples of a foggy belief window:

Julie was frustrated with her husband. Her main complaint: "There is always a high level of contention in our home. We argue too much. This yelling is affecting our kids." Steve, Julie's husband, did not agree with his wife. To him, they had what he considered normal relationships. Families have arguments, and yelling at your children is considered discipline. Steve had grown up in a home where his parents constantly argued. He had been yelled at as a child, and he felt he turned out just fine. He did not enjoy fighting with Julie but assumed this was how married couples co-existed. Julie knew there had to be a better way and begged Steve to go with her for counseling. Steve finally agreed. After multiple sessions with a counselor and a few group therapy classes, Steve began to see that his perception of family life was not correct. Many of the couples in the class they attended had found a deeper level of happiness and respect for one another. Once Steve experienced a new level of joy in his relationship and his children responded positively to his new way of parenting, he and Julie were able to make the necessary changes to improve.

When you honestly face your belief windows, certain truths may come forth that are difficult. It might be your child, a friend, a spouse, or a therapist who alerts you to a fallacy on your belief window. Be open and willing to unearth the pain, but be careful that the person in your life who is telling the truth does not suffer., especially if it is one of your children. This is described in *The Artists Way: A Spiritual Path to Higher Creativity*, by Julia Cameron.

> When people do not want to see something, they get
> mad at the one who shows them. They kill the messen-
> ger. A child from an alcoholic home gets into trouble

scholastically or sexually. The family is flagged as being troubled. The child is made to feel shame for bringing shame to the family. But did the child bring shame? No. The child brought shameful things to light. The family shame predated and caused the child's distress. "What will the neighbors think?" is a shaming device aimed at continuing a conspiracy of illness.[5]

However the truth comes to light, try to be grateful to the people and the situations that bless your life. Living new truths can make you feel uncomfortable, but with time, truth will bring freedom and happiness to your entire family.

As we finish this chapter on understanding ideals and pictures, it is important to remember the great worth of each individual. Show your children how valuable they are to you. Show them by understanding their needs. Watch them closely. Know their strengths and weaknesses. Ask yourself the following types of questions:

- Do their strengths lie within their schoolwork?
- Are they good at reading or writing?
- What subjects do they enjoy?
- Are they musically inclined?
- Do they have a tough time sitting still at a desk all day?
- Are they comfortable with friends, or do they struggle getting along with classmates?
- Are they good relating to and conversing with people?

Be realistic. Don't put upon them the strengths you wish them to have. Through your close attention, you will get the answers you need and get to know your child.

Give your children help when they struggle. When they are frustrated working on a math assignment, sit next to them and help. Even if you are not capable of solving the math problem, sitting close will calm down the child, eliminating the "I can'ts." Remind your child of the things they are good at accomplishing.

Help them understand that no one is good at everything. We all have strengths and weaknesses. Every individual has areas in which he or she struggles, and it is through these struggles that we become strong. Explain this concept to your children. Watch, help, and then stand back and observe. Remember, your job is to lift them up when no one else will. Love yourself and your kids, just as you and they are.

As an old man walked the beach at dawn, he noticed a young man ahead of him picking up starfish and flinging them into the sea. Finally catching up with the youth, he asked him why he was doing this. The answer was that the stranded starfish would die if left under the morning sun.

"But the beach goes on for miles and there are millions of starfish," countered the man. "How can your efforts make any difference?"

The young man looked at the starfish in his hand and then threw it to safety in the waves. "It made a difference to that one."

CHAPTER FOUR

Behavior

When a baby is hungry, she cries. When a toddler spies a toy he wants, he takes it. Right or wrong, pleasant or not, these actions make up what we call behavior. Behavior is actually quite simple to understand, but sometimes, as parents, we make it far too complicated.

Understanding behavior is key to parenting. Gaining this understanding is how parents can best learn the needs of their children.

Do you know how your child will react in a given situation?

Do you understand why?

Comprehending the patterns of behavior in our children will not only let us know how to help them, but this knowledge will greatly improve the Safe Haven we have been diligently working to create. Using behavior to understand non-verbal communication works for all ages, even adults.

When you are struggling to strengthen a relationship with your child, behavior is the missing piece needed to solve the puzzle. Behavior will be your red flag when something is wrong. Behavior gives obvious clues when you are trying to understand what is going on inside your child's head.

Most of us are good at paying attention to behavior only when it is bad. For example, what do you do when your son takes crayons and creates his own mural on the bedroom wall? What can be done for the child who throws temper tantrums in front of the candy counter at the grocery store? Or maybe your daughter borrows your scissors to gives haircuts to all the kids in the neighborhood. As your children get older, this bad behavior usually transfers into more serious acts, such as a teenager who borrows the car before he is licensed to drive.

When our children exhibit bad behavior, our first reaction is usually one of anger. Anger is a parent's most common reaction because it puts an immediate stop to the unwanted behavior. Anger is not a positive response. Anger will not change the behavior; it will only put a temporary end to the negative actions. The behavior will eventually resurface in another form. Anger does nothing but cause the bad behavior to escalate. Why? Your child's behavior is an exhibition of a need that requires fulfillment.

Instead of using anger on your child the next time you observe undesirable behavior, stop and dissect what is happening. Analyze the behavior. By this, I mean figure out what happened and why it happened, and consider possible solutions or changes.

Children who color on the walls with markers are not only curious but also testing their creativity. In their worlds, they are creating masterpieces. They are so intent on what they are doing that they have no concern for the angry reaction this might bring from a parent. As a parent, you are immediately upset with what you see on the wall. The thought process of a parent goes something like this: *What is my child thinking?! Who would make such a mess on a freshly painted wall? Why would Tommy do something like that? I have got to teach him a lesson so this will never happen again.*

On the other hand, the young child is thinking that the walls look much better now that he has added a little color. In his mind, he has taken a boring wall and made it "pop." It does not matter to your child that white walls might be what you prefer at your home. A child has his own perception of what looks best. If your reaction is one of anger, your child will be confused. Before you get angry, understand what your child is thinking. Get down on the same level with your child and look into his eyes. The innocent look you will find in his eyes should help tame your anger.

The moment you discover your child's *objet d'art,* you need to ask yourself: *Why did this happen?*

Tommy's behavior is showing you something about Tommy. Tommy has an interest in art. He needs somewhere to express himself. Wouldn't it be more productive to take Tommy to the art store and buy an art pad for him to color? Tommy's behavior is pointing you in the direction you need to proceed. Once the art pad is in place, then you can give your child a very simple and short explanation that the walls in your home are not there for him to color. Without using anger, you have freed yourself from any damage you could possibly do to Tommy's psyche later on in life.

Do you see how uncomplicated that was? Yes, it is your responsibility to remove the marker from the walls, but realize this is one of the hazards of having children. If you can control yourself at this stage of the child-rearing game, pat yourself on the back. You may now advance to "GO." Collect two hundred dollars.

It helps us all to know that we are not alone when mini-disasters (like marker on the wall) occur. These situations happen in a variety of forms to all parents. I had a son grab me by the hand and pull me into a room. He had just finished an entire mural on one of my freshly painted walls. He exclaimed, "Look how beautiful I made this room, Mommy!"

Thank goodness he was so busy admiring his work that he did not see the look of horror on my face. I had to calm myself down and ask myself, *What good would anger do at this moment?*

I regrouped, complimented my son on his artwork, and quickly purchased big sheets of paper he could use for his murals. Thank goodness the paper satisfied his needs, and he never again colored on the wall.

Now let's move on to our young hairdresser cutting her friends' hair. Most neighbor moms are not thrilled when their children have been given haircuts at the hands of another child. Your sweet beauty school prodigy will never be safe from the wrath of another mother. When this happens, quickly make your apologies to your neighbor, promising it will never happen again. Take your neighbor a plate of cookies and then purchase a doll with long hair your daughter can cut. You can find plaster heads at the beauty supply shop that come with long hair she can braid, cut, or, if you want to explore deeper, color.

Your child is capable of understanding a simple explanation that she can never again cut her friends' hair . . . or any other child's hair in the neighborhood. She now has a doll to practice on. No punishment is necessary—just the explanation.

Please note that although your child shows a current interest in becoming a beautician or an artist at this early stage in life, she has not chosen her final profession. Children will try a variety of options as they continue to grow and change throughout their lives. Your job is learning to understand the behavior and finding a solution to your child's needs.

If your child's behavior is plagued with frequent tantrums, it could be a sign of hunger, exhaustion, or frustration. Get food, lay your child down for a nap, or talk your child through making a choice. A child standing in front of the candy counter, unable to pick which candy he wants to buy, needs help learning how to make a decision. Talk them through it. Discuss which candy he chose last time, whether or not he liked it, or if he would like to try something new. This process takes time and patience.

Remember that it is from these simple decisions your child will learn how to make big decisions later on in life.

A teenager who takes the car for a joy ride without a license is showing you he has a strong desire to learn how to drive. You can choose to become angry, threaten, and punish, or you can take him to a parking lot and teach him how to drive. Drive with him until he can no longer stand it. If you continue to give your child as much driving time as possible, his desire to take the car without permission will soon disappear.

The key to improving behavior is not through punishment. It is through behavior that you learn of your child's needs. When you punish a child for bad behavior, you are punishing him or her for having needs. That isn't right. Most parents believe that without punishment, their children will become juvenile delinquents.

Children do respond to discipline, but the response you get from discipline is not the response you want. Children often react to discipline by repressing their needs, internalizing their negative deeds, and believing they are bad. Another common reaction comes in the form of rebellion. When you discipline behavior or what we have now labeled as their needs, your children will rebel against the authority figure giving the discipline. The reason they rebel is because you are stopping them from getting what they want. Neither of these solutions provides positive development for your child.

When you encounter behavior that is unacceptable, you must first understand why the behavior is occurring before you attempt to alter it. If you are able to treat the behavior with a practical response that meets the child's needs, then you will see a change in the behavior.

It is more important to teach a child the behaviors you do want as opposed to spending time teaching what you do not want, so illustrate the behavior you want. Create a plan for him or her to follow, and then praise your child when he or she emulates the positive behavior. Children need to hear praise more than they need to hear criticism. For every negative comment that slips out of your mouth, you will need to immediately say at least three positive statements to your child. It is much easier to never utter those negative statements.

When a child does well, you want your child to repeat this positive behavior again and again. This praise not only improves the behavior of a child, it strengthens the depth of the relationship between parent and child.

Look for the good in your child's behavior. Accept that your child is in the developmental stages, and react positively to your child's behavior. Never belittle your child for her behavior.

Most of us, when we see our children misbehaving, have formed the habit of doling out a threat to stop the behavior. Does this sound familiar? "If you kids don't stop fighting, you will be sent to your room."

Or, "If you don't clean your room, you will not be allowed to hang out with your friends tonight."

Focus on deleting the threat from your sentences.

"Kids, stop fighting" is all that needs to be said. Then play with them, redirecting their energies and their boredom. How about this? "Let me help you get started on cleaning that room." Then help them. Yes, this type of parenting takes more of your time, but in the end, it is worth the results you will get. If at the moment you don't have the time to help them, keep your mouth shut. Do not threaten, because it does no good.

The concept of not punishing a child for his or her behavior will be difficult at first. This practice, like the others we have discussed, will take time for you as a parent to master, but if you give it a chance, it can be fun trying to figure out solutions that answer the interesting behaviors your children present to you.

While you are working on this theory, it helps to understand a bit about human nature. A book I love, *Attention Deficit Disorder: A Different Perception*, written by Tom Hartmann, simplified and improved my understanding of human behavior. This book should be in the hands of every parent. Do not let the title of the book deter you from reading it. I strongly suggest reading this book in its entirety because Mr. Hartmann is much better at explaining behavior than I, but let me expound on a few of his concepts.[1]

In his book, Mr. Hartmann describes our earliest ancestors and how two basic types of cultures evolved. Mr. Hartmann originally proposed the Hunter/Farmer theory to help children and adults learn more about themselves: who they are, where they came from, and how they learn. These survival mechanisms have been handed down from ancestor to ancestor.

Scientists have since come forth with evidence that there are many truths in Mr. Hartmann's theory.

In tropical areas of plant and animal life, hunters and gatherers predominated. The traits they possessed made it possible for them to survive in their environment. Many of the same traits and characteristics used to describe hunters and farmers still exist today within us and in the behaviors of our spouses and children.

Hunters need a certain set of physical and mental characteristics to be successful in their surroundings. Failure to be totally aware of the environment could mean no food for the day or possibly even death. A rustle in the bush implies danger: a lion or a coiled snake. For a hunter, it is imperative to be flexible and have the ability to change direction in an instant.

Hunters often describe their actions in terms of pictures rather than words. They love the hunt but are easily bored by mundane tasks. Hunters have incredible bursts of energy. They get a thrill out of confrontation and enjoy facing challenges and even danger. Hunters are risk takers. Entrepreneurs, trial attorneys, and police officers are typical hunters. People labeled with ADD are usually hunters.

In contrast to a hunter, a farmer is not easily distracted by his environment. He is best at providing sustenance. To a farmer, it is important to sustain a slow and steady effort. Farmers understand the long range picture. They are excellent when attending to detail and not easily bored. Farmers are patient, cautious, and make good team players. They do well in school. The skills of a farmer are quite different from those of a hunter. Examples of farmers include teachers, bank tellers, and computer programmers.

Most of us will have a mixture of hunter/farmer personality traits. It is important to understand that both character types are necessary in today's society. It is also imperative to realize that these characteristics are an inherited set of skills or abilities. We cannot change them. As a parent, note how ill-suited a farmer can be in a hunter's world. Hunters, too, struggle to comprehend a farmer's lifestyle.

Many jobs in the workforce require a farmer mentality. You must show up for work at a certain time, do a task for a determined number of hours, go home, and then start all over the next day. Our schools are set up along farmer lines: sit quietly at a desk, ignore the child next to you, read a book, and answer the questions. Many parents and teachers label the child who fits the farmer's role in school as a "good" child. The hunter child who cannot conform and finds the school regiment difficult is labeled "bad." It is important as a parent to understand your child's traits so he does not spend much of his life feeling like a square peg trying to fit into round hole.

After reading Mr. Hartmann's description of these personality characteristics, you probably have a pretty good idea of the attributes you identify with. Do you recognize which traits are befitting to your child? Some of us will have varying degrees of both skills, but we usually tend to relate more to one or the other: the farmer or the hunter. It is important as a parent not to decide that one type (yours) is the best. Both personality types are important, and they both have a set of skills that will help children be successful.

Once you understand your child's behavior, you are much better equipped to help your child adapt. It is essential to note that you cannot change your child's behavior choice. Accept it and realize that, from this behavior, you will be taught how your child learns. This knowledge is imperative to understanding how and why your child reacts to life.

Both personality types, hunter and farmer, have strengths and weaknesses. Because our children are individuals, no two behaviors will be exactly the same. Some children are calm. They take life as it comes and not much upsets them. A calm child may not accomplish as many tasks but is able to focus on one responsibility and do it exceptionally well. She may even problem-solve along the way, saving herself from many disasters or failures. The downside is that because she moves too cautiously, she is unable to accomplish all that needs to be done.

Some children are extremely driven. They know what they want out of life and go after it. They have strong opinions and are not afraid to vocalize how they feel. They may not focus their attention on one goal but rather on multiple goals. This type of personality is exciting to watch but may move too quickly and carelessly.

Once again, you cannot change your child's basic personality traits. Ingrain that in your mind. Your responsibility is to take those traits and direct your child. Show him his strengths and gently warn him of how his weaknesses could affect him. As your child grows and matures, he will go through many changes, so be patient as he learns to understand who he is and how he works. Many of us as adults are just now discovering our own individual characteristics.

There are a few things to be aware of: for example, it is tough when a hunter child is put into our farmer-type schools. When a child's parent does not understand her behavior, it is easy for the teacher of a hunter child to point fingers and tell parents that there is something wrong with their child. If no one is defending the child, the odds are strong the hunter child will not succeed. Our prisons are loaded with hunter children who were never given the help and understanding they needed.

A farmer child who gets nothing but praise at school will excel. His trial may come in another area of life where he is not as confident. He may be verbally abused by a coach for not being able to think quickly and respond in an athletic competition. It is important in either situation to be protective as a parent. Do not let your child's self-image be distorted.

I hope you find this information from Mr. Hartmann helpful in your understanding of children and behavior. Armed with this information, it is time to observe your family's behavior.

This time, look for physical signs. An easy place to begin your observations is how they dress themselves. Clothing that may be driving you crazy could be the current rage at school. Go to school and take a look at what the kids are wearing. If your child's clothing is within the school's dress code and appears to be similar to the other kids', relax and don't let it annoy you.

You may notice that the manner in which your child is dressing is not the norm. For example, wearing all black could be a sign that something is wrong. "Gothic" clothing can be related to negative feelings, death, and drug abuse. The children who get caught up dressing so darkly on a daily basis are usually trying to find a place to fit in with a particular group of friends who accept them. The darkness signaled by black clothing may indicate loneliness, sadness, or low self-esteem. Heavy black eyeliner, black lipstick, and black fingernail polish represent an element of the rock 'n' roll music culture, but they also may show all sorts of sadness on the inside. Drug abuse is often a companion to this look, so watch your child closely. If you see signs of anger or depression, get professional help quickly.

If your daughter is wearing short skirts or low-cut tops, you have been given a clue that she has figured out a way to get attention from boys. Once again, your response should not be one of anger or forbidding her to wear that type of clothing. If she wants to wear clothes you disapprove of, she will find a way. Her behavior is telling you that now is the time to gently teach her there are other ways to get the attention she wants from boys. It is also a good opportunity to discuss the difference between types of boys. The boys who give her attention from wearing skimpy clothing might not be the kind of boys she wants. This is also a perfect time to remind her of the other worthwhile talents she has to offer.

Sometimes the way your kids dress is showing you that they may be crying out for more attention from their parents. Children need plenty of hugs and other signs of physical affection as often as possible from both parents. Even if you are not a touchy family, know that all children need affection. Wouldn't it be better if your child got the hugs she needs from you rather than some boy with raging hormones?

As you continue to observe the varieties of behaviors in your home, allow yourself to be taught by your children. Behavior doesn't just tell you when something is wrong; it also lets you know what you need to teach your child. If you are not paying attention, you could miss the feedback your child is giving you. Your child will move quickly through that stage in life without getting your valuable input.

As parents, it is easier at times to ignore behavior. Sometimes we don't see it. We might not understand it. But most times, we just do not want to deal with it. If you ignore negative behavior, it will get louder until you do notice it. Just as it is a lot easier to weed a garden before the noxious weeds invade, if you keep up on your child's life from an early age, you won't have huge messes to clean up later.

Children are not born with self-control. Self-control is a learned behavior and, over the years, can be mastered with experience. A child's behavior is motivated by both the strong pull of his inner needs and the pressure of outside expectations. It is unrealistic to expect a child to be perfectly behaved all the time. How many adults do you know that have this conquered? Children need to continually be taught and re-taught.

When your child exhibits behavior you don't like, keep in mind there is a good possibility he learned it from you. We all have issues. Much of our journey through life is spent learning how to overcome those problems. Most kids' issues have come from well-intentioned parents. So, without trying, it is inevitable that we will pass some of our problems on to our kids. I know it doesn't seem fair, but we *are* able to give our kids many of the good traits we possess. Unfortunately, the bad ones are part of the package.

You may not even recognize the problems passed along until you see the negative behaviors that arise in your children. No one wants to acknowledge their weaknesses—it would be less painful to have a tooth pulled—but sometimes there is no better way to understand our children than to look deeply into our own lives.

A great philosopher once referred to the problems we find in our lives as simply a bucket of manure. When we stir the manure, it stinks, but eventually the smell goes away. Yet, when we leave it alone, it will pile up. When I come upon a difficult issue that I would rather ignore, it helps to think of that "stinking manure" piling up. I'd rather deal with the temporary smell and get the problem solved. I just hope the smell leaves quickly.

Unfortunately, we pass many of our problems on to our children before we take the time to resolve them. Now take your problems, add your spouse's issues (positive and negative), combine that with your child's personality, and you will find you have created a very unique individual. This is your child. It is your responsibility to assist her. Help her understand her heritage, both the good and the bad. You may first have to do a little work with your own life and dig deep into your own behavior. Once you understand it, with or without counseling, then you are capable of helping your child.

We all have behavioral issues to decipher, things like childhood anger, jealousies, fears, insecurities, neglect, dependency, shyness, and dishonesty. There are a multitude of problem behaviors, too many to list. Pick the issues that hit closest to home. When you improve your own life, you will see your child's life improve.

Let's use anger as an example. How do you feel when it is *your* five-year-old who hits another child for getting in front of him in the school lunch line? Or when your preschooler has a screaming fit when a friend borrows a toy? For children, one of the most difficult developmental tasks is learning how to express anger appropriately. As a parent, the first thing you must do is figure out what is going on underneath all the anger. When children are angry, it is often because they don't feel loved, understood, or heard. Get down on their level. Look them in the eye and listen intently to what they are saying (or screaming). Sometimes if a child knows that a parent is willing to listen to her point of view, he will calm down. Your children need to know that you are there for them. Hug them, hold them, or just sit with them until they can calm down. Then, when they are ready, discuss possible solutions to their problems. They may just need to vent about why something is not fair. Your calmness will show them that there is someone on their side, someone who cares. Remember, they have probably learned anger from watching you. But just as they have learned anger from you, you can now teach them how to appropriately deal with that anger. Teaching a child how to handle anger comes from example.

Your example of handling your emotions will have a greater impact on your child than anything you say or do.

Understanding the role behavior plays in your home life will help you bring about improvement. As you read the following examples, probe into your own life, getting rid of those behaviors that are causing damage. Keep the conduct that will influence your children positively.

Deception

The Barton family was a well-respected family in the neighborhood. It appeared to be a happy household where life ran smoothly. The parents had been married for many years, and their children were high-achieving, popular kids. Mrs. Barton was active in her church and the community. She was a good person but never saw anything wrong with stretching the truth, especially if it made her family look good. She struggled with being totally honest—especially with herself.

She bragged to her friends about her children's accomplishments, sometimes making them sound much grander than they actually were. She enjoyed offering information on her financial status, dropping tidbits about her husband's salary and inflating the amount. Mrs. Barton had grown up in a poor neighborhood, and having money was important to her. It meant a lot to Mrs. Barton to have people think highly of her. She received a large sum of money from an injury sustained in a car accident. She was injured, but the injury was nowhere near as serious as her attorney portrayed it. Her part of the deception was easy. All Mrs. Barton had to do was wear a neck brace to her court case. The Barton family and their attorney received a large sum of money after winning the case. They were able to easily rationalize why they felt justified in going through with the lawsuit. Sadly, over the long term, they paid a bigger price.

This problem with dishonesty eventually showed its ugly hold in the Bartons' third son, Trevor. In the beginning, Trevor's dishonesty was evident with small acts. Trevor was capable of being a good student, but he didn't like homework. If he didn't want to open his books in the evenings, he lied to his parents by telling them he had finished his work at school. He even went so far as to brag to his parents that he never had homework because he was one of the smartest kids in the class.

Soon his grades began to suffer, and the school began to call home with complaints about Trevor. He made excuses to his parents, rationalizing that his teachers were against him. This behavior carried over into other aspects of Trevor's life. When he did poorly in sports, he knew if he could fake an injury, he would not be held accountable for his performance. The injuries got him out of school and gave him access to plenty of pain medication. As he grew older, he lied about his drinking, stealing, and eventually his heavy drug abuse. The path he continued to follow led him to fines, jail time, and then rehab. His life continued in a pattern of arrests, lies, and counseling, followed by continual attempts to straighten out his life and work through many of his problems.

You may think it harsh to blame Trevor's chosen path of life upon his parents, but where do you think Trevor learned that deceit and lying were an acceptable way to get through life? Children watch their parents. They imitate what they see. Trevor observed how his parents handled difficult situations and then took it a step further to a level that is not socially acceptable.

Neglect

Sadie was raised by a mother who worked full-time as a physician. Debbie (Sadie's mother) loved her daughter but was required to work long hours, and there were not enough hours in the day for Debbie to spend time with Sadie.

As a child, Sadie was lonely. She suffered from neglect. Barely out of her teens, Sadie found a solution to her loneliness by marrying young. She got pregnant early and quickly surrounded herself with many children. Sadie was no longer lonely. Sadie loved her children but repeated many of the same patterns of mothering she had learned growing up. She busied herself with many activities and was never around to spend time with her children. The kids were never neglected. They were well taken care of by nannies, but their mother, Sadie, was always too busy to give much of herself to her kids.

Sadie's children also longed for attention. Throughout their teen years it was the norm to have a boyfriend. Three of her children married young. The youngest did not marry but had many difficult relationships. It was a vicious cycle, started by an emotionally absent parent.

People Pleaser

Dave was a people pleaser. He didn't like contention. He became extremely nervous when he saw problems arise with his children. He avoided facing troubling situations by pretending they didn't exist. Dave was the son of a politician. His father was mayor of the small town where Dave grew up, and the entire town loved Dave's dad.

Dave emulated his father's positive attitude. Dave was warm and friendly to everyone in town but was very demanding of his own family. Dave wanted his children to present themselves in a positive way; he wanted model children. When his children had problems at school, he was uncomfortable believing and supporting his kids. Dave did not want anyone in his community to think less of him. When his children were involved in difficult situations, he immediately assumed it must be their fault. He always agreed with the teacher or the adult in charge.

Dave's children did not like how their father handled these incidents. The oldest son was full of anger. He felt abandoned, knowing his father would never stand up for him. He rebelled by spray painting graffiti on his dad's office building. Dave's middle son became shy and insecure, never able to look an adult directly in the eye. Dave's daughter and third child imitated her father, trying to please and never cause contention. She became pregnant during her teen years, trying to please the boys she dated.

One thing all three children had in common was prolonged unhappiness. This unhappiness made it difficult for Dave to hide his disappointment in his kids. With the sad looks on their faces, Dave's children were an embarrassment to him.

In each of the above situations, the parents were using learned behaviors as their methods to raise their children. It is a very natural thing to do and probably the only way most of us know how to parent. We seem to fall back on the parenting skills of our parents. It is common to react and raise our children just as we have been taught by our own parents. Good parents are not perfect. Many of the flaws in our lives end up becoming the norm in our homes because we were raised with them.

Let me again refer to Thom Hartman. In another book, *Beyond ADD*, Thom explains how this happens, sometimes unconsciously:

> The mind organizes itself into separate and discrete areas
> to deal with life's circumstances. These areas are created,
> organized, and segregated from the conscious mind
> during childhood for the largest part, and represent much
> of what is often referred to as "the unconscious." They
> work to keep us alive and protected, but because so many
> of them are created during childhood when cognitive
> abilities aren't well-developed (regardless of age), they are
> developed at the level of instinct. These areas of the uncon-
> scious that control much of our conscious behavior often
> appear to act in an irrational fashion.[2]

If we understand where our parenting skills originated, they are easier to analyze. Parents should be able to identify the methods they are using either as uplifting and beneficial or as harmful and damaging. This helps especially if you remember how you felt when your parents used those same tactics on you.

Even with all the knowledge you can muster, it would be difficult to break apart every single behavior you have as an adult. We may not even be able to comprehend why we react the way we do. In fact, we probably don't even consciously think about most of our reactions. Improvement comes when we can acknowledge that we are doing it wrong. Then it is important to believe these behaviors are either preventable or can be changed.

You have to be an example and model the behavior you desire. Children are too bright to be told to do one thing while they watch you do another. Be honest with your kids and in your dealings with others. Tell the truth. Admit to your children when you make mistakes, and apologize for those mistakes. Tell them when you are frightened as a parent and why. Apologize when you get angry. Explain to your children what upsets you and why. Admit to yourself petty jealousies. Support your kids all of the time. Do not hide your emotions from your children. They will respect you more if they understand the real you.

Julia Cameron quotes Margaret Young in her book *The Artist's Way*:

> Often, people attempt to live their lives backwards: they
> try to have more things, or more money, in order to do
> more of what they want so that they will be happier. The
> way it actually works is the reverse. You must first *be* who
> you really are, then, *do* what you need to do, in order to
> *have* what you want.[3]

Model the behavior you want, and when you see your child exhibiting the behavior, name it to your child. "I appreciate your telling me the truth."

Repeat this process again and again. Help your children do the things you want them to do. Show them; do not criticize. Compliment them when you see them modeling this behavior.

"Children Learn What They Live"
—Dorothy Law Nolte, PhD

> *If children live with criticism—they learn to condemn.*
>
> *If children live with hostility—they learn to fight. . . .*
>
> *If children live with ridicule—they learn to be shy. . . .*
>
> *If children live with shame—they learn to feel guilty.*
>
> *BUT*
>
> *If children live with tolerance—they learn to be patient.*
>
> *If children live with encouragement—they learn to be confident.*
>
> *If children live with praise—they learn to appreciate. . . .*
>
> *If children live with fairness—they learn justice.*
>
> *If children live with security—they learn to have faith. . . .*
>
> *If children live with approval—they learn to like themselves.*
>
> *If children live with acceptance and friendliness—they learn to find love in the world.*[4]

The best answer to improved behavior is *example, example, example*. If you haven't been the greatest example over the course of your child's life, it is never too late. Begin now! Children are quick learners. If you can always keep in mind that parents are continuously under scrutiny by their children, you will strive to live your life in a nobler manner.

We are examples to our children in everything we do. We often do not realize how our idiosyncrasies are passed onto our kids. Erma Bombeck explains:

> There is no need to wonder how little girls grow up to be fastidious, nit-picking, domestic perfectionists. They are groomed that way. Several weeks ago, I heard from

children who had been raised by "The Speed Demon," a woman obsessed with cleanliness. The children had some concern about their futures.

This prompted a letter from "Raked But Not Ruined," four sisters who said their mother, Donna Reed, not only vacuumed the rug every day, she raked it. If you made the mistake of walking into the living room, you had to rake your way back out. They revealed she once extinguished the pilot light on the water heater as she was vacuuming it.

The scary part about all of this is how growing up in this antiseptic environment ultimately affects your life. The "Raked But Not Ruined" heirs say . . . "When you least expect it . . . you develop an uncontrollable urge to clean the insides of electrical outlets. One bright, sunny Saturday morning you wake up with no other thought in your mind than scrubbing your baseboards with a toothbrush. You are never safe. You have to force yourself to leave some crumbs under the toaster."[5]

If you find you cannot change all of your quirky behaviors, you can at least acknowledge and laugh about them. This humorous act alone will give your kids the option for change.

There are some behaviors we worry about that are normal and natural in most kids. While we are trying our hardest to be the best parents possible, we sometimes overreact. Earlier in the chapter, I used lying as a negative example. I may have frightened you into thinking that even the smallest lie could lead directly to drug abuse. Let me caution you to not overreact, especially when young children are involved.

John Rosemond, a family psychologist, enlightens us about kids that lie.

> All kids lie. Telling an occasional lie and being a liar are two different things. All children lie at one time or another.

However, few children actually become liars. Young children, especially preschoolers and early elementary-age kids, often stretch the truth. . . . [These exaggerations] happen because the child has a rich imagination . . .

Kids who lie habitually generally lack a sense of accomplishment. Lying fills this void and develops into a game. Don't give a child a chance to lie when you are reasonably sure of the facts. . . . By asking a child a question to which you know the answer, you are actually setting the stage for a lie. (Of course, when you're truly uncertain about the facts, you have no choice but to question the child and then decide whether he or she is indeed telling the truth.) The more children are punished for lying—especially if the punishments involve physical pain—the more they will try to avoid being punished again. It makes sense that a frightened child is more likely to lie. . . . Remember, don't let a lie distract you from whatever it is that the child did wrong. The great storyteller Samuel Clemens, a.k.a Mark Twain, once said: "When I was younger, I could remember anything, whether it had happened or not."[6]

Most of us feel it is our responsibility to punish for the lie. Once again, since we are trying to understand the behavior, you don't need to get angry over the lie. It is more important to understand why the child needed to lie.

What Really Matters

David is four years old. While playing, he saw a toy he liked that belonged to his friend John, so he took it. John wanted the toy back, and David refused to give it to him. John went to David's mom and told her that David had taken his toy. David hid the toy under the couch cushion and lied to his mom, telling her he had not taken the toy. His mom was quite sure David had taken the toy. She confronted David in anger, accusing him of stealing the toy. David was frightened, so he continued to lie, denying he had taken the toy. His mom became so enraged that David would lie that she literally backed him up against the wall while she interrogated him. David was crouched in the corner crying, "I didn't take it, I didn't take it."

Towering over him, David's mother's response was, "Just tell me the truth David. I don't care if you took the toy. Please, just don't lie to me!"

Can you see the nightmare occurring in this confrontation? David's mother is so concerned that her son is lying she has forgotten about David and what is going on with him. She is worried that she needs to stop David's negative behavior immediately. David's mom needs to stop, step back, and remind herself that this is normal behavior for a four-year-old. The mother is overreacting to the situation, and damage is being done to the child. This is not the time to verbally attack David. This is the perfect opportunity to teach.

Let's go back, understand the behavior, and then watch as the response changes. Our four-year-old David spies a new toy, and he wants it. His desires are so strong that he is unable to understand that he cannot just take the toy. David's mother could begin by getting down to eye level with her son and gently explaining to him that the toy belongs to someone else. She needs to acknowledge how fun the toy is and tell him that she understands why he would want to keep it for himself. David is old enough to comprehend that his friend would feel badly if David kept the toy. Her voice should be calm and quiet and filled with love.

This is a teaching moment. It is also an excellent time for her to tell her child how much she loves him. She should then explain how she trusts him to give the toy back to his friend. Then David's mom needs to step back and give David some space and the opportunity to give the toy back on his own. It may be necessary to repeat this conversation again and maybe a third time. At some point, David will understand and give the toy back to its rightful owner.

This opportunity is not only teaching a child not to steal or lie, but showing your child the trust you have in him. You are also teaching another

---

important lesson to your child: how to get along with friends.

It is in these small, impromptu moments that we do our best teaching. The little things become the big things which make up our family tapestry. We want that tapestry to radiate love. If you can stay calm, observe behavior, understand that behavior, and finally react using love and patience, you will be successful. This method works with four-year-olds, fifteen-year-olds, and forty-year-olds!

I want to share a story relayed by Harold B. Lee, a prominent religious leader. Think of this young pilot each time you encounter a problem with your child. It reminds me of how vulnerable we all are when trapped in a difficult learning experience. The officer in the story shows us how to react correctly to behavior.

> A young pilot in a solo flight high above the airport in a training routine . . . suddenly shouted over the radio communicating system to the officer in the control tower: "I can't see! I have gone blind." Should panic have prevailed in the control tower as well, disaster to the young pilot and to the valuable plane would have been certain; but, fortunately, he was a seasoned officer who, from experience, knew that under certain circumstances temporary blindness could come to a young novice under great tension. Calmly, the officer talked to the youth up there, directing him in the process of circling to lose altitude slowly while at the same time ordering emergency equipment to be brought, at once, should there be a crash. After breath-taking minutes which seemed interminable to all who watched, the blinded pilot touched the wheels of his plane to the runway and rolled to a stop on the landing field. The ambulance attendants hastily rushed the boy to the base hospital for treatment.
>
> What would have happened if the officer in the control

tower had become excited or had been shirking his duty, or hadn't known how to deal with this kind of an emergency? The answer is that the same thing would have happened which could happen to [a youth] were she bereft of the wise counselor of experience when she is faced with a shocking crisis with which she is unaccustomed. In both instances, a life would be maimed, if not destroyed, and the opportunity for highest attainment blighted.[7]

As parents, we are the experienced officers, and it is important for us to have the ability to calmly talk our young pilots through the turbulence and larger emergencies they encounter. It is during the daily experiences we have with our children that they form the confidences they need to successfully make it in this life. Never give up on a child—even if he is defiant. There are still ways he can be reached, somehow, someway, sometime. Pay attention to the behavior. It will always lead you in the right direction.

CHAPTER FIVE

Control

Throughout time, we as a human race have been inflicting dominance on what we consider the "lesser" members of our society. As far back as Adam and Eve, control has been an issue. Cain used control to gain Abel's flock of sheep. The Egyptian Pharaohs wielded control to dominate Moses and the Hebrews. What is this obsession our society has with power and control?

Control is a major problem in our families. Control creates battles between parent and child and causes an immeasurable breakdown in family communication. *If we want to be successful in our families, we need to find a compromise with control.*

All of us, at some point in our lives, have personally invoked control or been the recipient of control. Control is so commonplace we often do not recognize when it is being used on us, nor are we able to stop ourselves when we attempt to control others. Control comes in a variety of forms, some of which include manipulation, domination, and exploitation. Whatever you want to call it, *when you take away someone's rights or freedoms, you are using control.*

Control has become such an accepted form of behavior that it often becomes difficult to recognize its use. Yet it is simple to determine control with one statement:

When people refuse to hear and/or respect you when you say "NO," they are using control.

Control takes away choices. As parents, our pursuits should be to present all possible options and solutions to our children and then let them make their own choices. If you start this process at an early age, while teaching correct principles, the decisions your children make when they are young will not be monumental or disastrous. When your children get older, the mistakes they need to learn from are more serious. Your child's punishment might be in the form of a ticket or an arrest. The process of stepping back and letting your child make choices cannot be established without trust. With that trust, you hope they will make the right choice. Difficulties with trust arise when the wrong decision is made and we must let our children learn from this decision.

Control exhibits its ugly face when we are too frightened to let our children make their own choices. As a parent, when you step in using control, you will destroy trust in the relationship. Not only does control take away trust in the relationship, but children will seldom ask for your advice or respond to your requests.

Using control is a very common, yet frightening, technique of getting what you want as a parent. It happens quickly and is hard to stop. As parents, when we try to control, we are not doing it to enhance our child's needs. We are usually doing it to protect our own needs. As with blame or anger, when you use control on your child, you will pay dearly for it.

Many parents get frustrated with the fact that their children often do not agree with their points of view. As a parent, don't you just love it when your child takes your advice without dispute? When dealing with teenagers, it is normal for them to have different opinions. Teens are learning independence. It is part of the growing up process. Children will not always agree with their parents because they have different needs. Survival as a teen is pretty tough these days, so it is important to allow our children to have as much independence as possible.

In the previous chapter on behavior, we discussed the farmer and the hunter. When you have the combination of a farmer parent and a hunter child, you often have serious control issues. Control can escalate to frightening levels, depending on the strength of the personalities involved. Mr. Hartmann warns us in his book: "Beware the over-focused Farmers, who want to set the rules and define the game."

Be extremely careful of the rules you set in your home. Analyze each one of them, and discuss them with your children. You can frustrate a child with too many rules that have been set to control. It is a possibility your hunter children might explode from the pressure of too many rules. Give your children choices. For example, let them decide when they will get up summer mornings. Let them choose what they will wear to school or what food they will eat. Give them more choices than rules.

Let me show you how easy and commonplace control can be:

Emily and her mom fight about hair every morning before school. Emily wants to wear her long hair down and loose—not tied up in a ponytail. Emily loves the feeling of her hair flowing behind her as she runs at recess. She has a friend who wears her hair down, and Emily likes the look. Emily's mother feels strongly that Emily's hair looks much better combed back tightly in a ponytail. It is such a nice, clean look, and it keeps her hair from getting tangled and falling in her face while she does her schoolwork. Emily's mom struggles watching Emily leave for school in the mornings with that "wild hair." So every morning, like clockwork, there is an argument about Emily's hair. Emily finally gives in, letting her mother slick that hair straight back into a ponytail. Emily's mom hates the arguments but gets satisfaction from

Emily's meticulously combed hair and from herself being in control.

Must our need to be right as parents be so all-consuming? Mom has won this battle, and she feels a satisfaction of sorts that continues to drive her to the next encounter. But mom is refusing to see what she is doing to her daughter. How do you think this will affect Emily in the long run? Shouldn't Emily's feelings of self-worth be more significant?

Sometimes, as a parent, you must stop yourself and analyze your reasoning for control. Ask yourself why certain decisions have to go your way. Is it important that Emily's mom appears to be a good mother to other parents because of the way her daughter looks? Or is she obsessed with a particular image she wants Emily to model? If Emily's mom could listen to and respect Emily on these small issues like hair, as she grows older, Emily will be more inclined to include her mother when bigger issues arise.

Don't ruin your relationship so you can feel in control. Adults who fear they will not appear to be good parents are falling into a control frenzy. It is imperative to block this behavior. Deepak Chopra, MD, states it clearly. This advice applies to not only mothers but fathers as well.

> For most of us, the person who loved us most dearly was
> our mother, but if you reflect on it, this love often implied
> power and control. As a child, you had to do what your
> mother said or her love might be withdrawn. "I'm your
> mother, you have to pay attention to me" is the opposite of
> "I love you, and my greatest happiness is to see you become
> what you want." The first statement may come from love,
> but it is not a love that easily permits freedom.[1]

Emily is young. She will go along with her mom for now. But as she gets older, somehow, someway, Emily will rebel against her mom's control of her freedoms. Whatever her choice of rebellion, it likely will surface in a form that elicits the most anger from her mom. At that stage in Emily's life, few will be able to understand Emily's anger. Emily may be labeled a bad child.

This story is all too common. We witness the rebellion of children who come from good homes. From an outsider's position, we find the situation baffling. It is difficult to figure out what happened or why. In most cases, the problem arises from the controlling behavior inflicted by a parent. It is difficult to admit we use control. So parents often defend their positions with statements that go something like this: "If I am not in charge of my child, he will never learn to be a responsible adult," "I refuse to be the parent of one of those out-of-control kids," "I am just teaching my child responsibility," and finally, "I always know what is best for my child."

If you realize you have said those very phrases or even something similar, stop yourself from using control immediately. Remind yourself that your greatest happiness aligns with what Mr. Chopra stated: "to see your child becomes what he wants."[2]

Forming a United Front

Even if there is only one parent using control, it is the responsibility of both parents to stop this behavior. If your spouse is the one exerting control, your job to protect the child becomes imperative. You have to step in and stop the control. It takes two adults, with different viewpoints and behaviors, to protect a child. As parents, you do not always have to agree with one another to thrive. In fact, the most successful parents have regular differences of opinion.

When you are in the heat of battle with your child or even just involved in a minor disagreement, it is much easier for the parent viewing from the outside to present a fresh point of view to the argument. The outside parent is capable of suggesting alternative solutions to solve the problem. It is unfair to join together as parents and rally against a child. Why is this unjust? Because you are taking away the hope for justice your child has. Additionally, you are leaving your child with no one to turn to for help. Your child is void of an adult to discuss a different opinion with.

Forming a united front has often been considered a necessity in parenting, so this concept will come as a surprise to most parents. Many parents also struggle with the concept of stepping in and stopping a spouse who uses control. If the child is to be protected, this must be done.

It is always best, as parents, to discuss the difficulties your child is facing before the problem erupts. If this is not possible when problems arise, it might be necessary to physically put your body between the controlling parent and your child. You cannot allow this behavior to continue. *When you have a controlling parent, there is always damage to the child.*

Be careful in making the decisions that affect your child. *Do not mess around with control.* I cannot state this more strongly. The results are painful. Using control does not bring about a change in behavior. It creates resentment that will be aimed directly at you. Children respond negatively when you try to control them. Remember Newton's law: for every action, there is an equal and opposite reaction.

Parents often get stuck in a role of being "The All-Knowing." You do not always know what is best for your child. Sometimes, as parents, we are right, and sometimes we are wrong. Being wrong is not the problem. You have already learned the importance of listening to your children and paying attention to their opinions. The problem arises when our child disagrees or says "no." Then, instead of hearing them or trying to understand, we figure out a way to get the child to comply. Why do we continue doing this when we know it isn't right?

As parents, we get stuck using control because it works quickly and easily. When you use control, you can make your child comply immediately. Once you are in a pattern of using control, it is difficult to stop.

When a child is forced to comply with a parent, the most common reaction from a child will be to defy the parent on another issue. When a parent sees this defiance or rebellion, he tries to exert more control, and the child, in turn, responds equally with more rebellion. It becomes a vicious cycle that escalates until the child's behavior is completely out of control. *When the behavior your child is exhibiting is rebellion, there is too much control in your home*—and not enough support.

It is frustrating as a parent when your child won't do what you want, especially when you know it will benefit her. To help you clearly understand this concept, I need an illustration that continually causes frustration in homes. How about schoolwork and grades?

Most parents become upset at the end of the term when their children bring home report cards with low marks. It is frustrating as a parent to have a child do poorly in school. This frustration leads to anger. From the anger comes control. Control displays itself in the form of punishment. The student is threatened that the grades had better improve or he will be punished. This punishment is designed to make a child work hard and never bring home another bad report card. It could be a weekend of nonstop studying, a driver's license taken away, or the dreadful reprimand of grounding.

Grounding, to a child, is a horrible punishment. It can last for a week, a month, or until the grades improve. I have known kids who have been grounded for an entire school year. While we are discussing reprimands, I wish someone could explain to me what punishments like grounding have to do with the low grades. This punishment is not discipline. Grounding is a form of control.

Let's analyze this situation and figure out how we can solve this problem without falling back on the use of punishment to control. The problem is grades—low grades. As a parent, the first question you must ask yourself is, "Why is my child not doing well in class?"

To answer this question, you need to begin a fact-finding mission to gather information. First, go directly to your child. Calmly, giving your child the benefit of the doubt, ask, "What do you think the problem is?"

Carefully *listen* to the answers she gives. Do not pass judgment on whether or not she is telling the truth. Just listen.

With modern technology, we have many ways to decipher the truth. Look up grades on the internet so you can get a clearer picture. Are there missing assignments? If so, find out which ones and why. Could it be that the assignments have been turned in and misplaced? Maybe your student forgot to put his name on the paper. Is the problem poor test scores? Throughout this thoughtful interrogation, you are not judging your child, just gathering information so you can make an informed decision.

Next, put on your detective cap and go talk with the teachers involved and get their input. *Do not take your child with you.* No child should have two adults finding fault with him at the same time. If all the teacher can do is criticize your child, you have a big clue as to why your child is not doing well. The teacher has already decided there is no hope for your child. Once again, remember you are not placing blame. You are on a fact-finding mission.

Go back to your child and calmly discuss the information you have received. During your investigation, make sure you are not angry, hungry, or tired. Try to be in an upbeat frame of mind. Listen to the responses you get from your child. If the child does not understand the subject, like math, help her. She may need help. If you are unable to help, get a tutor. When you approach the problem in a factual manner without anger or emotion, you will discover the answers. As your child witnesses the time and effort you are willing to devote to her education, she, in turn, will try harder to improve.

No Need to Be the Enemy

Throughout this process, you should become an ally with your child, not the enemy. You will know you have not used control to solve the problem if you have remained the ally. These experiences build stronger relationships with your child. If you think it sounds like a lot of time and effort, you're right. Asking a child to handle this situation on her own is too much responsibility, because she does not know how. She will learn how to handle an experience like this from watching you.

By becoming involved, your child knows you care and that she is important to you. It also lets her know that you are willing to help. The benefit that comes from your involvement in tough situations like these is that your children get to witness you, the main adults in their lives, learn how to solve the problem. You are teaching them. You will be pleasantly surprised when they eventually gain the skills to do it for themselves in the future. It is important to remember that a child cannot go up against an adult without the support of another adult. It is not a fair fight.

All too often, I hear parents say that their children need to be responsible and take care of these types of problems on their own. If they knew how to do it, they would. Sometimes, the reason that we are uncomfortable helping our children in sticky situations is because we never had that example in our own lives. Most of us never had parents that did this for us. We may not feel capable, so we shy away from it. This is the time as a parent when you need to step up to the plate and go to bat for your children. The earlier in their lives you begin to assist them, the sooner they will be able to do it alone.

It is important for your children to learn how to control themselves. I believe the best place for them to be taught is in the home by their parents. Children have been observing their parents since they were born. They have learned the majority of their behaviors from you. No one is going to love your child as much as you do. No one is going to understand your child as much as you can. You are the best person to teach them self-control. Don't relinquish your parenting responsibility. Some parents find it difficult to tolerate mistakes made by their child and feel their only option is to let someone else parent their child through difficult times.

As I was writing this chapter, a story in the *Oakland Tribune* caught my eye. A fourteen-year-old boy was sent by his parents to a camp for troubled youths. The boy, frustrated and frightened, sent a letter to an adult friend who then questioned if the parents of this child had the right to exert this type of control, and a lawsuit ensued. Unfortunately, the lawyers will now be the ones making the decision instead of the parents.

"Frustrated Parents Have Teenage Son Abducted"
(Oakland, California)

Two burly strangers came in the middle of the night and took sixteen-year-old David Van Blarigen away because, his parents say, he was unhappy at home. When David eventually arrived at a Jamaican camp for troubled teenagers, his banishment raised a difficult question: was this tough love or not enough love? Prosecutors say it looks like kidnapping to them. They plan to go before a judge . . . to argue that David should be returned home for a hearing on his welfare. But to their supporters, parents James and Sue Van Blarigan are heroes who were willing to take drastic measures to avoid releasing a troubled teen into the world. "Where is a parent going to turn if you take this away?" says Tim Flood, who credits a camp similar to the one the Van Blarigans chose with saving his own son from ruin. "If I were a parent and I could not do this kind of thing, I would give up because I can't do anything to control the peer group. That's way too powerful."

Neil Aschemeyer, a neighbor who went to authorities after getting a collect call from David in Jamaica, says the boy has never used drugs or alcohol and has exhibited little more than typical teenage rebellion. Aschemeyer, an administrative law judge who has known David for about six years, says he felt compelled to act when David called and told him, "This place is like a prison. I want to come home."

Dan Koller, the Van Blarigans' attorney, says Aschemeyer misinterpreted the phone call, which David made from the airport in Jamaica's Montego Bay before he

even got to the camp. Recently, David has written positive
letters to his parents, Koller says: "He's understanding how
he took everything for granted." The attorney says it would
be absurd for a court to stop parents from sending their
children to camp or school they may not want to attend.
Koller says David once had been suspended from school
and was failing. . . . But Aschemeyer says David's problems
at school were minor. He says the boy has attention deficit
disorder but was interested in doing well at school, particularly in algebra. Aschemeyer also says Mrs. Van Blarigan
had complained that David didn't show his parents proper
respect. He says the boy had quarreled with his parents,
who are devout Christians, over church attendance.

Prosecutor Robert Hutchins told *The Oakland Tribune*
he believes the parents sent David to Jamaica because they
were taken in by a high-pressure sales pitch. Hutchins'
petition to bring David back was filed in civil, not crimi-
nal, court. He told the newspaper that regardless of their
motives, parents don't have the right to have their children
abducted. Minors older than fourteen can refuse to go
somewhere, he said.

When David called Aschemeyer, he said he was taken
away November 10. He said the two men sent to do the
job threatened to handcuff him, locked him in a car, and
drove seven hundred miles to Brightway Adolescent
Hospital in St. George, Utah. He was locked in a facility
with youths with alcohol and drug problems, Aschemeyer
says. From there the teenager went to Tranquility Bay, the
Jamaican treatment program."[2]

How do you feel about this story? We each may have a different reaction to this story. Some may agree with the Van Blarigans, saying there was

a problem and they immediately dealt with the situation. Others will be appalled that a fourteen-year-old could be treated in such a manner. The parents appear to have good intentions but are not getting the behavior they want from David.

What they want in David is a child who goes to church, a child who doesn't argue, and a child who gets good grades. Isn't that what every parent wants? Wouldn't it be easier on all of us as parents if our children did everything we told them?

Instead of watching David's behavior and trying to figure out what the catalyst might be, David's parents relied on control and set themselves up as the enemy. This example illustrates how using control is a quicker method of getting an immediate response from your child. When you use this kind of control, input from your child is not necessary. Look at the results they got. David is now behaving—not because he wants to, but because he knows if he doesn't, his parents may have him kidnapped again. This manner of discipline is not parenting.

Why did David show a lack of respect for his parents? In the previous chapter, we discussed how to get the best solution: *pay attention to the behavior.* The answer lies in David's behavior. David was struggling in school. He was not doing well because he had learning disabilities. David needed help. If you were not doing well in school, would you want to be there? No! So David ditched school.

If David's parents had paid attention to the fact that he had a learning disability, they could have saved themselves a lot of money. It would have been far less expensive to pay for private help for David's ADD than to ship him off to Jamaica. If children hate school, there is a reason.

Controlling Control

One way to stop control is by listening. Listen to your child. When your children say "no" to you, don't get irritated with their disobedience. Figure out why. A child will listen when you try to explain your side of the equation—if you stay calm and listen to her. If you are truly listening, you won't use control. Make sure you let her explain her position. There's nothing as desolate as thinking the person you're closest to does not understand you or is not trying. Take time to think about what they have said to you before you arrive at a decision, but always listen.

Giving someone your undivided attention is an art—an art we knew as children but seem to have lost as adults. As babes in the womb, before we could see or taste or feel anything, we could listen. In the past few years, there has been a sharp decline in listening. There are too many ways to attract attention and take the focus away from listening to our child. Our culture is a noisy culture, and we are bombarded from every direction.

Slow your life down. To understand your child, you must slow down and listen. Parents in a hurry do not take the time for their children, and their children feel it. It can sometimes take sitting for hours until a child feels comfortable enough to open up and let you listen. This is not an easy task and is especially hard in today's fast-paced lifestyle.

The art of therapy is the art of good listening. Olga Silverstein, a family therapist, says:

> Good therapists listen with the third ear. That means listening for more than what is said, being able to hear underneath the words to the real content. Every sentence has a meaning beyond the one that is manifest. If you believe there is such a thing as the unconscious mind, then you have to elicit that information. You listen and then you facilitate further revelations by the questions you ask rather than the comments you make.[3]

Conflicts arise in families because each conversation contains a message (the literal meaning of the words) and a meta-message (an unspoken meaning conveyed through the tone or the history of the relationship). We must learn to respond to the meta-message and hear the words our child cannot say without superimposing our own assumptions on our children's actual words.

Be aware how you respond to particular people or topics. If you catch yourself having a negative reaction, you can stop and ask yourself, "Was I listening to the real words that were spoken? Is this a reasonable response to what this person has just said?"

Deep listening with a finely tuned ear is a gift you can give to your child, but it does require practice and skill. Learn how from a few experts. Here is an interview with Alan Ross. All he does is listen. He is the executive director of Samaritans of New York, a suicide hotline.

> The best listeners, he says, allow the other person to open up. This doesn't necessarily mean listening silently, though. He suggests that when you do talk, you ask open-ended questions like "How are you dealing with this?" instead of yes or no questions, such as, "Do you really think you should let things go on this way?" "The latter kind of question is really a judgment," Ross says. "You're not asking—you're telling someone what you think." Instead, Ross says, "Shut up. That's what I tell myself every time I think I have something to say. Stop and put the focus back on the other person. . . . The real payoff is not that the person will walk away with answers to life's problems but that she will feel validated.[4]

Holly Mullen writes about a teacher who listened and made the difference in a troubled teen's life:

> She could have cut. She was so close to slicing into her wrists, letting the blood flow as she drifted quietly away to a place she felt sure was better than this one. . . . [Rebecca] gives credit for her decision to hold on another day to one

man: Brent Jepperson, a fifty-two-year-old journalism and
creative writing teacher at Bonneville [High School]. . . .
Rebecca tells her story of surviving three suicide attempts
to social workers, corrections officials, church groups—
anyone who works with young people and anyone who
will listen. . . . When Rebecca, a lovely woman with porce-
lain skin and brilliant eyes, testifies to the power one adult
can have on one troubled teenager, there is no doubting
her story. "He let me talk. And talk," she says of Jepperson,
who helped her design her own course of study her senior
year. "My parents tried hard to help me, but this teacher
did three things that no one else had done: He respected
me, he trusted me, and he treated me as an individual."

"Kids' families are being destroyed. They feel alienated,
ignored, disposable," says [Jepperson]. In Rebecca's case,
her family was intact, but her self-esteem was not.

"I told her quite simply, 'If you don't drop out, I won't.'"
She did not. She graduated in 2001, and now assists with
art and music therapy in a Davis County Schools. . . .
"Becca," as Jepperson calls his former student, was unique
in her own right, and yet her story is sadly replicated every
day by children crying for help, but who simply slip away.
Jep did not let this one get away.[5]

Listen closely to what your child is telling you, but do not judge. I know it
sounds simple, but listening to your child is the first step in stopping a cycle
of control.

Are there other ways to stop yourself from using control? You, as the parent, have to make a commitment to change. If you want to control something,
control yourself.

In an interview, J. Keith Miller, author of *Compelled to Control*, gives us
excellent insight to control:

The control factor is an insidious force in relationships, creating resentment and bitterness. . . .

"The discovery that I had a compulsion to control everything and everybody in my life came as a real surprise to me," he says. "I had always seen myself as a sensitive person who wanted everyone to be free to do what they needed and wanted to do.

"What I didn't see," Miller continues, "was that my controlling presence was like a giant amoeba that slowly spread over my intimate relationships, oozing silently and inexorably across other people's boundaries, until my vocation, my ideas, and my expectations crowded out the space for their identities and growth.

"My controlling behaviors were somehow occupying their emotional territory. Instead of focusing time, attention and love on them, *my* life had become the central life in our relationships. My vocation and dreams absorbed my thinking and took up the space where their lives would have been free to develop. . . .

"Intimacy means that I share my *personal reality* with you—especially my thoughts and feelings—*and you do not "fix" me*, or try to adjust my reality by telling me that I 'shouldn't feel' what I have expressed. Then you share your personal reality with me, and I do not fix you." . . .

Control issues "slam the door on intimacy," for "who wants to share their reality with someone who's going to point out what's wrong with it and you in the process?" Miller emphasizes.

When the need to control becomes a compulsion, and thus an addiction, those who control may need the same kind of twelve-step program utilized to aid people with other addictions, stresses Miller. . . . He says:

1. Concentrate on your own control issues. Lay aside the issue of fixing the relationship and focus on fixing yourself. Recognize that the need to control has to do with your need to feel secure.

2. Let people make mistakes without penalty. "Making mistakes is how everyone learns about life. . . . I have always been compelled to note their failures for them—just in case they might miss them. I noticed how angry and silent or rageful they got, but I couldn't understand why they were so upset, since I was 'just trying to help.' . . . I see now that I tell them about their mistakes as a way of controlling them, suppressing my fear of not being adequate." . . .

3. Give up needing to "win" or "to be right."[6]

Many parents feel that everything in their lives will fall apart if they don't control. David Viscott, the author of *How to Live with Another Person*, talks about individual rights in an interview. When you use control, individual rights are compromised. Every living being has rights that you need to respect.

> A person's individual rights in any relationship are the same rights he enjoyed before he even knew the partner existed. Rights are not to be bargained for. They simply exist. A relationship's task is to recognize and protect the rights of both parties.[7]

To Viscott, these include:

- The right to grow, to achieve the fullest potential, and to seek happiness as each defines it. A relationship should never become a jail, holding a soul hostage for a ransom of love which is conditional on a person's always staying the same.
- The right to be oneself—to be the person he is, the sum total of his

feelings, thoughts, affections, tastes, dislikes, and perceptions.

- The right to be loved, to be accepted, cared for, and adored.
- The right to privacy—to a private life, a private world of her own, time alone to be accountable only to herself. This includes places where she can see friends, have conversations, and maintain cherished interests, hobbies, amusements, and sports.
- The right to be respected—to have room to speak his mind, to be listened to, and to have opinions taken seriously.
- The right of acceptance—the right to be wrong and to make good a mistake; to have her apologies accepted and her love cherished in the spirit it was given.
- The right to be free—to be allowed to follow his feelings, the dictates of his heart and his good sense.[7]

These rights and freedoms are imperative to a child, so respect them. Control issues are tough. It is usually quite difficult to recognize control in yourself. A spouse or a dear friend may be able to alert you when you become too controlling with your child. If you find you are struggling with issues of control and are unable to moderate your behavior, get professional help. If you control now, you will pay for it later.

It is important to remember that growth takes place from the decisions we are allowed to make. If a child's choices are taken away, the growth will disappear. No parent likes to see their children fail, but sometimes they must fail to progress. Childhood is the time for trial and error. When they blow it, let them fail with dignity. Don't rub it in, saying, "I told you so."

There are many areas in a child's life where parents use control. Robert Kirby, a columnist for the *Salt Lake Tribune*, wrote an article about what to do when your child chooses a different religious path. The piece has more to do with control than religion.

> It can be a painful experience when someone you love doesn't live his or her life according to your expectations.

That's right. Let's not kid ourselves, OK? The pain we feel sometimes has more to do with a personal loss of control than any real notion that our loved one is lost forever. Forever is God's business. Human beings have a hard enough time figuring out current events. One of the great ironies of religion occurs when worry over the next life screws up this one. . . .

Lots of frantic parents seem perfectly willing to destroy a relationship with a child over the issue of church affiliation.

How do we do this? Easy. We just let our disappointment speak louder than our love. We become the prod in prodigal. Pretty soon, Junior isn't running toward anything so much as he is running away from us.

But what do we really do? There has to be some way guaranteed to save Junior . . . Well, actually, no. This is his choice, not ours. Our job is not to make the situation worse. There are [a] number of things we can do to keep that from happening.

First, we have to shut up. Junior already knows how we feel. Twenty years of mandatory Sunday school attendance made that perfectly clear. . . . Second, we treat Junior's girlfriend kindly, even if she has a tattoo of a snake on her forehead. We don't improve our relationship with him by undermining theirs.

Next, we stay involved. Even if Junior's girlfriend turns out later to be a boy, we maintain contact in a positive way.

Remember all that boundless love and long-suffering stuff we wanted Junior to learn in Sunday school? It applies to us, too. Now is our chance to prove that we were paying attention.[8]

As your children get older, you will realize that it is not control you wanted from your children. What you need from your children is for them to learn the skills of self-control. Ironically, learning these skills comes from practicing freedom of choice. Once they master this, they will take control of themselves. Parents and children should work together to set the standards in the home. Children want and appreciate limits. They need them, but you must set them together. You will have more success in developing self-control in your children if they are involved in making the decisions and setting the limits.

CHAPTER SIX

Motivation

Most parents want to know how to motivate their children. The answer is simple: it begins with trust and ends with protection. Trust between parent and child is a wonderful thing. You have mastered the key to motivation when you value this trust with your child and never allow it to be compromised. Motivation results from the reverence we have for our child's free agency. Does this mean parents are responsible for their child's level of motivation? Most emphatically, yes!

A child's motivation is sacred, and it needs to be protected. Parents are responsible, or should I say accountable, for protecting their child's dreams. *Motivation is a combination of lifting your child as far as she will let you and protecting that child on whatever path she chooses to follow.*

Each child is different and has a unique style to approach life. Individuals are inspired in a variety of ways. Julia Cameron tells how she motivates in her book, *The Artist's Way: A Spiritual Path to Higher Creativity*. Julia has a fascinating job. She motivates artists. Julia works with artists who are "blocked" and unable to create.

Although most of the examples in her book are for adults, I found that many of her ideas apply to children. When a child has no motivation, he shows the same symptoms as an artist who is blocked. They are often frustrated, not knowing how to get started, or frustrated that the results of their efforts are not perfect. Giving up is an easier path. Children, like adults, often need help finding their passion and also need reassurance that their efforts are good enough.

> I have worked artist-to-artist with potters, photographers, poets, screenwriters, dancers, novelists, actors, directors— and with those who knew only what they dreamed to be or who only dreamed of being somehow more creative. I have seen blocked painters paint, broken poets speak in tongues, halt and lame and maimed writers racing through final drafts. I have come to not only believe but know:
>
> No matter what your age or your life path, whether making art is your career or your hobby or your dream, it is not too late or too egotistical or too selfish or too silly to work on your creativity. One fifty-year-old student who "always wanted to write" used these tools and emerged as a prize-winning playwright. A judge used these tools to fulfill his lifelong dreams of sculpting. Not all students become full-time artists as a result of the course. In fact, many full-time artists report that they have become more creatively rounded into full-time people.
>
> Through my own experience—and that of countless others that I have shared—I have come to believe that creativity is our true nature, that blocks are an unnatural thwarting of a process at once as normal and as miraculous as the blossoming of a flower at the end of a slender

green stem. Our creative dreams and yearnings come from a divine source.[1]

If our motivation or creativity is our true nature and whatever it is that is stopping us is an unnatural thwarting, what causes this lack of motivation? I think you will be surprised at the answer. *Don't let others set the standards by which you will succeed or by which your child will succeed.* It is easy to understand but a bit more difficult to implement. Julia says it this way:

> Teachers, editors, mentors are often authority figures or parent figures for a young artist. There is a sacred trust inherent in the bond between teacher and student. This trust, when violated, has the impact of a parental violation. What we are talking about here is emotional incest.
>
> A trusting student hears from an unscrupulous teacher that good work is bad or lacks promise or that he, the guru-teacher, senses a limit to the student's real talent or was mistaken in seeing talent, or doubts that there is talent. . . . Personal in nature, nebulous as to specifics, this criticism is like covert sexual harassment—a sullying yet hard-to-quantify experience. The student emerges shamed, feeling like a bad artist, or worse, a fool to try.
>
> Although we seldom connect the dots, many of our present day losses are connected to our earlier conditioning. Children may be told they can't do anything or, equally damaging, be told they should be able to do absolutely anything with ease. Either of these messages blocks the recipient.[1]

Whatever path your child chooses (business, math, art, dance, or athletics), whenever his talent is doubted, it harms motivation. Parents can, all too quickly, kill a child's motivation by yanking him into an adult world. Many grownups leave children in a disorienting world without an adult hand to guide them. This happens when we put them on schedules as demanding as a company president's, dress them up as beauty queens, leave them all day under the supervision of someone who doesn't love them like a parent, or simply sell their souls to the television. Children need your positive influence and guidance.

Where do you begin when your child is just not motivated to do anything? How do you go about motivating a child? First, you protect them by setting your own standards of success for them. Make sure they are getting positive feedback. Next, realize it is important to set achievable goals. This means knowing your child and her capabilities.

For example, in grade school it is common practice for children to be given a weekly spelling list of about twenty words. We all know that in a classroom there are many different types of students, all at individual learning levels. Some children will be able to spell all twenty words with ease, while others will struggle with five. With the different levels of learning, it is necessary for some kids to study for hours to pass the test. Sometimes, even after studying long hours, they do terribly on the test. Ask yourself this question: "Why do teachers, who should have a pretty good idea of each student's abilities, give them all the same test?"

The test does not meet each child's needs. If you were the student who fails the test, would you be motivated to study the next week's words? I doubt it. What if this same child puts aside his math homework and devotes his entire study time to focus on spelling and is still unsuccessful? Week after week, year after year, this child will dread spelling.

Remember, in this chapter, we are talking about how to motivate your child. Whether it is spelling, mathematics, or history, the key is to protect that motivation. To stay motivated, your child needs small successes along the way.

To understand this concept, compare learning how to spell with learning how to walk. We all did not learn to walk at the same age or the same speed, but we all eventually mastered it. Just as with walking, there is no decree declaring the day, hour, or minute that we must know how to read, write, or spell. There is not a timeline when it comes to learning. Children learn at their own pace and on their own time. If you push them too hard, they will become discouraged or fail.

To protect motivation, children cannot be overwhelmed. We should not give our children more than they can handle, or they will quit trying. The goal is to give them just enough to succeed, then introduce more as they are ready for it. It requires a bit more effort, but it is very doable.

If you are expecting a teacher to take care of the situation, it will not get done. The classrooms in our schools are far too overcrowded for personalized attention. But you, as a parent, can do this. How? Set achievable goals.

For example, let's go back to the spelling words. Work with your child and figure out how many words he can realistically learn in a week. Five? So work on five that week and then stop. I guarantee that if your child finds he can successfully spell five words, he'll ask for more when he is ready. You are not letting your child off the hook, and you are definitely not keeping him out of Harvard if he cannot spell all twenty words on that spelling list. What you are doing is helping your child succeed by breaking the learning into pieces he can handle. You are also protecting his motivation.

The next step is talking to the teacher. Gently but firmly explain to the teacher what you are doing and why. Tell your child's teacher that all your child will be learning this week is five spelling words. Depending on the teacher, you may have to reassure her that you will take full responsibility for your child's education. Offer to sign any form needed to release her from this responsibility. But do not let the teacher change your commitment to protect your child's motivation. If your child's teacher refuses to cooperate, you may need to request a new teacher.

Remember, if your child is forced to accomplish more than he can handle, over time it will kill your child's motivation. The teacher might make you feel guilty, saying that your child will drop behind the class. She may try and tell you that your child is capable of more but is just lazy. I guarantee that once your child tastes a little success, he will push himself. No one wants to fail, especially your child. When a child's motivation is intact, he will soar. Nothing can stop him.

Depending on the situation, whether it is educational, extra-curricular, or social, children all respond differently. They are individuals. If your child feels confident at something, she will step out or take the lead. If she comes back to you wanting reassurance or help, give it to her. Don't say, "You know how to do this," or, "Don't ask me for help," or "You are too old to ask for help."

Give them the help they need. They will take charge and move forward when they feel confident. Your child will let you know when he no longer needs you. This goes for spelling tests, math homework, sleepovers, sports, friends, and, down the road a ways, college.

Maturity also affects motivation. Many students struggle with going away to college right out of high school. It may be so difficult for them that they drop out after their first year. That same student may decide to come back a few years later and eventually find success. It takes success, even in the smallest dosage, to motivate or challenge a child to try new things.

As a parent, when you become frustrated with your child because she will not push herself to achieve what you think she is capable of, remind yourself that real love is believing in your child until she can believe in herself. Again, keep in the back of your mind, *there is not a timeline that fits everyone. Let your child progress through life as she is ready.*

Fear and frustration are also causes for lack of motivation. We can be paralyzed by fear. It stops us from stepping out of our comfort zone into new arenas. The practice of using fear tactics never works. Fear tactics kill motivation. When children are forced to try new things, they will not push forward but will instead pull away.

The opposites of fear and frustration are curiosity and excitement. Curiosity is one of the greatest factors in motivating a child to learn. Children become bored when they are continually exposed to the same teaching methods. Expose your child to new and exciting experiences, then let her step forward when she feels confident.

Patrick Welsh, an English teacher at T.C. Williams High School in Alexandria, has some great advice on motivation from a teacher's viewpoint:

> I've given up my old fear tactics. ("Your transcripts will follow you all your life" or "You won't get a good job if you can't write well".) They are enormous lies. I've had too many students who I didn't think wrote well but who are now very successful, and make three and four times my salary. I now tell my classes that not everyone can write well, but everyone can improve. I sometimes even reassure kids that if they totally mess up high school they can always go to NVCC. High performance there will help blot out a poor high school record. I'm not lowering my standards; I'm trying to set achievable goals. . . . We do our kids no favors when we transfer to them our own anxieties about surviving in today's competitive world.[2]

You kill motivation by pushing a child to make choices and aim for a goal that may not be in her best interest.

When children are young, they are loaded with motivation. If a child wants to learn something, you cannot stop him. As he grows and receives feedback from teachers, parents, and classmates, that motivation is altered. In Tony Morrison's novel *Sula*, she gave a description of how the lead character Nell's parents killed her motivation: "Her parents had succeeded in rubbing down to a dull glow any sparkle or splutter she had."[3]

Pay close attention to your child, and watch for a lack of enthusiasm. When you see the dull eyes, you will know that something or someone is killing your child's motivation. It could be a coach, a teacher, or even a parent, but someone is zapping your child.

It is impossible to protect your child all the time, but you can help: be positive, do not nag, help her discover her strengths, assist him with his schoolwork, protect her from overachieving adults, and do not let him take on more than he can handle comfortably. Too many high school students are overloaded with AP classes, homework, music lessons, and sports, and this is all alongside an already busy teenage life. Let kids have fun during their childhood. High school is still part of childhood. Remember, you only get one shot at each stage in life. Your children can never go back and redo this time. We all know there is plenty of adult life and stress yet to come. Let them be kids!

There is nothing greater than watching a child who is motivated and excited excel at something he is driven from the heart to do. John S. Tanner, an academic vice president at Brigham Young University, gave a talk to other members of his faculty that exemplifies this true motivation.

> "Anyone can become a dean, a professor, a department head, a chancellor, or a custodian by appointment—it has happened thousands of times; but since the world began, no one has ever become an artist, a scientist, or a scholar by appointment. The professional may be a dud, but to get any recognition, the amateur has to be good." [Hugh] Nibley aptly reminds us that true excellence comes not by appointment but by accomplishment.
>
> The word *amateur* derives from the Latin for "love." An amateur is at root a lover—a lover of sport, science, art, and so forth. . . .[4]

Tanner continues by reviewing two characters in the film *Chariots of Fire*, Harold Abrahams and Eric Liddell. Both were gifted sprinters and both won gold medals in the 1924 Olympics. Abrahams was the professional runner. He was driven, highly coached, and obsessed with winning. Liddell was the amateur. He ran from his heart—joyous, animated, and driven by the love of running. He says he runs for God. In the film, Liddell says:

> I believe that God made me for a purpose. For China. But
> He also made me fast. And when I run, I feel His pleasure.
> To give it up would be to hold Him in contempt. You were
> right. It's not just fun. To win is to honor Him.[4]

I love sports. It is through athletics I have witnessed many clear illustrators of motivation. Gordon Monson, a sportswriter for the *Salt Lake Tribune*, wrote an article about Coach Craig Poole, one of the most successful track coaches to ever coach.

Monson praises Coach Poole's refreshing philosophy:

> The man has spent his life learning to be a better coach. He
> has read hundreds of books and thousands of articles on
> the subject. He had an undergraduate and two advanced
> degrees in physical education. He has studied the ins
> and outs of motivating athletes, emphasizing the psycho-
> logical aspects of pulling the most out of them, over a
> thirty-seven-year career. . . . And you know what he says?
> . . . He says never be negative. He says coaches who are
> screamers and yellers and critics don't know what they're
> doing. He says put a happy face on every moment. He says
> coaches who regularly visit the past, who review film and
> break down their athletes' mistakes and drive them into
> their athletes' grilles, wayward coaches who berate those
> athletes in dramatic or traumatic ways, are reinforcing
> precisely what they want their athletes to avoid.
>
> He is a professor of sports psychology at BYU and
> the women's track coach. His success would be consid-
> ered ridiculous if it weren't so routine. His teams have
> earned ten top-10 finishes at national championships.

The women's cross country team, which falls under his direction, has won three national titles since 1997. He is considered the pre-eminent expert on heptathlons and heptathletes in the United States. Hence, his recent invitation to join the American coaching staff for the Athens Games. His techniques are refreshing and rare. . . .

"I don't permit the use of the word *can't*," he says. "When someone is beating up on herself, I tell her to give herself credit for what she's doing right. My job is to teach and motivate, and that's what works best. . . .

"I want every kid to have a good experience and to be better than she was when she leaves us," he says. "I want them to be a better athlete and a better person. I want them to take positive things with them that will last for a lifetime."

Coach Sunshine wants his athletes, then, to look straight ahead because looking back—at anything but a fond memory—is for negativists, chumps, and losers.

It's for coaches who don't know what they're doing, who haven't yet discovered the power of positive thought. Pity the fools.[5]

If only all of us as parents, coaches, and teachers who associate with children understood this philosophy and could grasp this positive aura. Coach Poole never criticizes his athletes for what they cannot do; instead he praises them for what they do right and builds from there. It is the athlete himself, not the coach, that motivates. We can use Coach Poole's process as parents. Praise and help your children to have enough small successes that they will gain the confidence to motivate themselves.

One more example is from the NBA. This again comes from sportswriter Gordon Monson writing about retired Jazz shooting guard Jeff Hornacek:

Storyline goes like this: Young dude grows up the son of a coach in a Chicago suburb, playing every sport known to young suburban dudedom. Baseball is his true passion. . . . Hoop is an afterthought, for good reason: He enters high school at 5-foot-2, 110 pounds, and leaves it at 6-2, 150. If teammate Bobby Hauch doesn't smash up his dad's car during school, and get himself suspended from the team, the little junior scrub known as "Horny" may not make it off the bench.

He does. Still, he's on the path to nowhere. Few college programs want him. He walks on at Iowa State, and gets a scholarship, he says later, "only because their other players kept flunking out."

College is good to him. He puts up nice numbers, and, as an accounting major, crunches more. By the time he's a senior, he meets a farm girl named Stacy, falls in love, and prepares for his fate—working as an accountant, quietly living in a tract home on a quarter-acre lot surrounded by a white-picket fence and beds of tulips and daffodils in Des Moines, Iowa.

Hold it. At the last minute he gets invited to play at a pre-NBA Draft camp. Jerry Colangelo, then the General Manager of the Phoenix Suns, is intrigued enough to make him the 46th pick of the '86 Draft. "Most of the people thought Jeff was not good enough to play in the NBA," Colangelo says, "But there was something special about him. He had a big heart." . . .

He makes it. . . . His touch becomes magical. He hits jumpers, runners, spinners, floaters, bankers, squibbers, leaners, game-winners.

The seasons pass, and over time he becomes a main

cog in Utah's [Jazz] playoff runs. . . . Because he uses brains
instead of speed or brute force, his effectiveness remains.
. . . "Thing is," Jerry Sloan says, "Jeff's a better person than
player." In him, perspective is everpresent.[7]

Even though many great athletes have support from friends and family,
the motivation to excel must come from within. Literally, motivation is the
desire to do. It is the difference between waking up before dawn to go to
swim practice or sleeping in. It is impossible to hand your desires and motivation to your child. They must figure out what they want, power through
the pain, and become who they want to be. You can help them. If you protect
your child's motivation and give them your support, you will influence their
desire to achieve more. That is the best way to inspire.

"Every blade of grass has its angel that bends over it and
whispers, 'Grow, grow.'" —The Talmud[8]

Motivation through Disappointments

Passion is a wonderful thing. Passion is what we are looking for in life: to find
what we want, and go after it. Thomas Edison said it this way:

"If we all did the things we are capable of doing, we would
literally astound ourselves."[9]

If you can find your child's passion and protect it, you will never have a
motivation problem.

It would be wonderful if our lives were filled with only passions, but
there are trials in life. Even when you find what motivates you, it seems there
are always stumbling blocks. Sadness and disappointment seem to surface
when we least expect. It is tough to learn how to handle disappointments, but
it is even more difficult to help our children cope. A child needs to learn how

to deal with disappointment so he does not lose his motivation. Dr. Joyce Brothers gives excellent advice in an article entitled, "When a Dream Doesn't Come True."

> Disappointment is an unfulfilled dream—a result of working hard and not achieving our goal. Regret is usually about something we didn't do, disappointment about something we didn't get. A major disappointment is something like a death—the death of a dream. So allow yourself to grieve. This is not the time to tell yourself, "I'll get over it," or, "After all, no one died." Instead, feel your emotions fully. If possible, talk with an empathetic person who has had a similar experience. The first step is to evaluate the disappointment: Why did it happen? Can you curtail future disappointments?
>
> How to avoid disappointment? Rate your expectations. Ground expectations in reality. Lighten up. Most of us are carrying far too many expectations. Let go of those created by society's demands: I should be financially successful, live in a great house, and be a great lover, slim and attractive—now and forever. Many of us strive to respond to standards that simply can't be reached. Make sure an expectation comes from deep within you and no one else.
>
> Jettison a sense of entitlement. Do you expect things to go your way simply because you're you? Reflect back on the disappointments you've experienced in recent months. If they're numerous, it may be because you're expecting too much. None of us is entitled to have all our dreams come true.
>
> Have "something in the mail." Producer David Brown always has a project on the back burner in case his current film gets canceled. Cultivate a wide variety of interests so

you can avoid being focused on just one expectation.

Resilience is the key to overcoming disappointment. "It is no use sitting upon me," Winston Churchill once said, "for I'm india-rubber [and I bounce]!" We have to bounce back. It's amazing how often the survivors of a disappointment say they ultimately wound up where they were intended to be.

Steps Toward Recovery From Disappointment

- Take care of yourself. As you go through the stages of grief, surround yourself with family and good friends.
- Go easy on yourself. Recognize that self-blame is not helpful. A study found that those who can admit a lack of control over events tend to recover more quickly.
- Take an inventory of the good things in your life. Write them down. Among your blessings, count the interests, skills, and activities you like. Realize that they are your lifelines to better times.
- Enjoy each day. Savor the routines that give you comfort. Smell the roses and tickle the daisies. They never disappoint.
- Understand that a disappointment can help to reinvent your life. "When one door closes another door opens," wrote Helen Keller. The key lies in developing a new set of expectations and making them just as valid as the ones that were lost.
- Laugh. Disappointment is oh-so-serious. Laugh at yourself, and its stranglehold will soften.[11]

Protecting your child's motivation is not that difficult if you follow a simple plan: Let your children learn as they are ready; do not push; break projects or assignments into doable pieces; help them discover something at which they can excel; when they fail, let them grieve through disappointments; and help them bounce back from failure. Realize, however, that the freedom to fail is the freedom to grow. If you are successful at everything you do, it might be that you are not challenging yourself. Finally, continually praise your children for their efforts.

CHAPTER SEVEN

Education

Our children enter an exciting yet challenging world when they walk
through the school doors on the first day of kindergarten. The education our children receive is an important factor in their development. While
the subjects they study are significant, the manner in which they are taught
greatly affects their attitude towards school.

Education is also a major factor affecting how your child feels about himself. His ability to grasp concepts, understand the material, and pass tests will
either catapult him to success or bruise his self esteem. As he works his way
through this process, it is natural for him to compare his own abilities to the
achievements of other children in the classroom.

Why is education such a challenge? At an early age, a child leaves home,
a place where everything he does is wonderful, to attend school in a large
classroom where he is thrown together with a variety of children from varying backgrounds. Then add a teacher who, in the eyes of your child, becomes

the ultimate judge of their abilities. It is an exciting new world for a child, but it can be tough. Will your child fail or succeed? Will he be able to keep pace with his classmates?

During the years of education, it is not possible to protect your child from many of the negative comments that will come his way. Life gives us many teachers—some caring and other cruel. Most teachers will be positive influences on the children they teach. Hopefully, when your child makes a mistake, your teacher will gently show her the correct way. Sometimes a child is humiliated or teased when she does not understand the correct answer or the right way to solve the problem. If your Safe Haven is in place, you can save your child's self-esteem by daily discussing the problems that occur at school.

When he leaves the nest, every child is introduced to a new environment filled with challenges. Depending upon their experiences and backgrounds, some children flourish while others struggle.

If we as parents are involved and part of the process, we place ourselves in the position to effectively help our children when they need it. It is for their own good that we cannot be with them every step of the way . . . nor would they want us around all the time. However, there are many ways to be involved. Your most important contribution to your child's education, as discussed in the last chapter, is to protect the motivation. It does not matter where a child's level of academic ability lies. Each child deserves to feel good about her individual abilities.

The Frustration Station

As you become aware of the importance of education, it is easy to become frustrated with the methods used to teach our children in our public and private schools. Thom Hartmann, in his book *Beyond ADD*, explains how and why our schools are set up the way they are. Mr. Hartmann's book was written for the parents of children with ADD, but pay close attention because his advice and knowledge will be beneficial for all.

According to Mr. Hartmann, many of our schools are doing exactly what they are designed to do: cause children to fail. This is interesting stuff:

> Give the average American Teenager a computer . . . and within a week he or she will have figured out how to find just about anything on the Internet . . . Try to teach the exact same skills, using the exact same equipment in a traditional school setting, and you'll have a year-long curriculum which will produce a healthy crop of failures.[1]

The origin of our school system dates back to the 1800s. Germans found that, to win wars, it was necessary to have soldiers who were willing to obey authority and take orders. A German philosopher, Fichte, proposed to create a "system of forced education which would produce soldiers and citizens who would be obedient, well-behaved, and unquestioning of authority."

Our children are graduating from high school without critical thinking skills. Students need to be able to think, not memorize. The school system is failing our children if we are letting talented children do the same thing day after day. They need to be challenged. If all we expect from our children is to be good test takers, be obedient, and not think or question, then we are not demanding enough of our schools.

Mr. Hartmann continues by calling for a radical reinvention of our school system with new solutions that include the following: relevant curriculums, student participation in the educational process, students' help in defining the rules of classroom behavior, good teachers being recognized and paid appropriately, and parents and community leaders breaking down the mandatory structures of education to open up more alternatives, such as charter schools and home schooling. Mr. Hartmann feels that the decision of education belongs "with the parents and communities, not with the federal government or even the state government."[1]

In American schools, we focus on content instead of technique. We seem to be obsessed with loading our children's heads with facts:

Children are taught to be organized, to do things in what's considered the proper fashion. . . . "We are so driven these days by tests and scores, by standardized levels of achievement, that we have little time to handle what I'd consider the basics: how to study, how to learn, how to get organized and do your homework. Classrooms are viewed as places to impart information, and therefore we've lost the concept of mentorship—of teaching *skills*. Education should be about lighting the fire of interest which will burn for the rest of the child's life, but instead we've made it just the filling of the bucket of a white-bread curriculum.[1]

After reading the information given to us by Mr. Hartmann, it helps us to understand why many children feel worthless and frustrated when it comes to school. They struggle to stay focused and will ditch school, fake an illness, or do just about anything to get out of it. Why? What has happened to these kids to kill their desire to learn?

There are multiple problems. The majority of curriculums offered today are boring. They do not create a challenging environment. Our children struggle in overcrowded classrooms. Students are overwhelmed with standardized tests, which also cut into the amount of time teachers have to teach. Negative consequences of so many tests include narrowing the curriculum, teaching to the test, pushing students out of school, and driving teachers out of the profession. Testing should not be the main focus of our schools. They do not show improved levels of achievement or the individual abilities of each child. If test scores and grades are low, children feel inadequate. I have often felt, while watching my own children go through the public school system, that it is frustrating when our schools cannot find avenues of success for each individual child. All of us are capable of learning and succeeding at something, but we must be allowed to do it in our own unique way.

It would be impossible, as parents, to overhaul the entire school system while raising our families. Yes, there are major flaws, and it is important to do what you can to improve the schools in your community, but if you are currently in the thick of raising children, the best, most immediate answer for you is to protect your own child. This requires getting involved in your child's education.

Understanding Learning Patterns

The best way to get involved in your child's education begins by your understanding how your child learns. Knowing his learning patterns is very important to academic success. Visual, audio, and kinesthetic/tactile are labels for certain types of learners. Many kids best use a combination of these learning styles.

Some children are visual learners. They can visualize a concept when they see it written on the chalkboard, and they will remember it. They may have difficulties focusing on a lecture if there are no visuals. Visual learners are often very artistic.

Others are audio learners. They need to hear lectures. They are very good at recalling instructions when they hear them. If the information they need to retain comes from reading, they may have difficulties remembering. Some need to hear the instructions and repeat them back to the teacher before they have a full understanding of a concept.

There are children who need both the verbal and the visual to comprehend directions.

Some kids are active and learn while moving. This learning style is referred to as kinesthetic/tactile learning. An active child thrives in an energetic, action-filled classroom. This child needs hands-on learning. A kinesthetic learner usually doesn't require instructions to assemble something. They are often athletically inclined.

Watch your child and try a variety of scenarios until you find the optimal learning environment for him This is not difficult; it just takes observation.

If you do a little research, you will be able to find additional information about many types of learning patterns. You can find free, online tests if you are interested in a more thorough understanding. Enter the words *learning patterns* in your search engine, and you will find numerous websites loaded with information.

Once you understand your child's learning patterns, it is important to explain your findings to your child's teacher. This is more difficult than it sounds. When you talk with your teacher, choose your words carefully, otherwise this teacher may assume you are there to criticize his or her ability. Teachers these days have so many children in their classroom that it is virtually impossible for them to individually help each child.

While working with my own children, I discovered my son could learn his spelling words much more quickly if he was jumping on a trampoline or playing basketball. When he sat still, his brain shut down. So when I helped him with homework, it was an active session. Fortunately, my son had a wonderful teacher in the fourth grade who, after I explained that he was able to learn more if he was moving, let him have a seat in the back of the classroom. He was allowed to walk about the back of the room when he needed to move. He was never allowed to disrupt the class, and he was always required to stay on task with his assignments. My son followed the rules set by the teacher while being allowed to move. He excelled that year in school. I will always be grateful to Mrs. Christensen for her willingness to adapt her classroom so my son could learn.

Some teachers do not realize that when they give an assignment, it needs to be written on the board as well as verbally told to the children. The best teachers do both of the above, along with sending home a list of assignments so parents can follow up. If your child is continually missing homework assignments, ask your teacher to do both.

A visual learner needs to use visual aids, like diagrams, when she studies. It will help her to take detailed notes during lectures and use color coding. It would help an audio learner to record lectures and listen to the tapes to study.

He can read aloud or study with a partner so he can talk about the main ideas. The kinesthetic learner should use flashcards she can move around. It would also help to take frequent breaks or move and stretch while studying. A kinesthetic learner would also be helped with color coding, reading aloud, and diagramming lecture notes.

All classrooms have students with a variety of these learning styles. Do not believe that your child is abnormal. It will be beneficial to discuss your findings with the teacher. There will be other children in the classroom who will receive help from what you do for your child because they learn the same way.

Be aware as you pursue your quest to improve the learning environment for your child. You will find most adults believe that it is the child who should conform to the institution. This does not work. Children will fail if we do not find a way to modify the system so it benefits each individual child. If you wait for the school to adapt to your child's learning style, your child will lose. Parents must get involved and help.

Instead of investigating learning patterns, many professionals and educators will suggest medication as the best solution for an active child to conform to a traditional school setting. Here is Mr. Hartmann's professional opinion:

> There is no doubt that medication can produce a huge difference in a child's performance in a public school setting, but many private schools obtain similar results by simply using smaller classes. This instruction moves at a pace commensurate with the child's ability to learn, and the teaching is in an active, visual, hands-on fashion . . .
>
> Over and over again on the ADD Forum on CompuServe, we see parents complaining that their ADD-diagnosed children are acting-out in school more out of boredom than anything else. "My son reads five grade levels above his class," one parent commented. "He spends most of his time in class trying to sit quietly while the

teacher is holding the hands of the slower students. It's no wonder he gets bored and fidgets."

The teacher's prescription, of course, was to medicate this woman's son. While that would have helped him sit in his seat for the entire class day, and thereby increased his grade scores, it would have done nothing to address the fact he was ready to learn more than the teacher was able or willing to offer.[1]

Parent volunteers work wonders in this situation. When you have an overcrowded classroom, another adult in the room can take a small group and move with them. It doesn't matter which group the extra adult works with, whether it is the slow kids who are struggling or the kids who need to be challenged. The analogy needed here is "divide and conquer." Offer to organize individualized learning groups for your teacher.

Holly Robinson illustrates how we have to trust our own instincts when we are trying to understand our own child's learning style in her article, "Are We Raising Boys Wrong?" As you read this article, do not forget that this does not just apply to boys, because many girls struggle with the same issues.

> In the opening pages, of Mark Twain's classic novel *The Adventures of Huckleberry Finn*, Huck explains how tough it is to live in a house with the Widow Douglas, who is intent on "sivilizing" him. Finally, says Huck, "when I couldn't stand it no longer I lit out."
>
> We all recognize and love Huck as the classic "boys' boy" who hates captivity and craves adventure, the riskier the better. So here's the question: If Huck Finn were a real kid and alive today, would we love him just as much? Or would he be hauled in for testing, diagnosed with Attention Deficit Hyperactivity Disorder (ADHD), and dosed with Ritalin? . . .

Most elementary schools give boys very little leeway to be themselves—particularly if being themselves involves classic "boys will be boys" behavior, such as competitiveness, aggressiveness, outspokenness, or endless motion.

Consider, for example, the fact that we still expect our six- to eleven-year-old sons to sit for hours at a stretch, reading or writing, at a time in their lives when adventure calls. . . . Boys at this age are on a developmental rung that requires stabs at individualism and independence. Yes, boys *will* be boys—because they're wired that way. It's unfair to hold them to a standard they aren't designed to meet. . . .

Thirty years ago, for instance, unsupervised play was a routine feature of childhood: Kids went outdoors after school and burned up excess energy by playing tag and climbing trees. But today, free-for-all childhood time has been steadily replaced by organized after-school programs, or, for the ever-swelling ranks of latchkey kids, a dizzying range of electronic diversions. Boys now have few places to tussle and race. At many schools, even physical education and recess have been dramatically cut back. . . .

Unfortunately, we've been going for the quick fix. When boys don't adapt, we're prepared to medicate them until they do. The drug of choice is usually Ritalin. . . .

Can this pathology really be that prevalent? Absolutely not, says Thomas Armstrong, PhD, a former special-education teacher and author of *The Myth of the ADD Child* (Plume, 1997). "Simply put, what teachers are calling ADHD today is often what we considered 'all-boy' behavior thirty years ago," says Armstrong. . . . As Armstrong points out, ADHD is a disorder that "pops up in one setting, only to disappear in another." Up to 80 percent of kids with attention disorders, he says, don't appear to have them when they're engaged one-on-one with adults. Nor do they show excessive hyperactivity or impulsive behavior if they're free to choose learning activities that interest them and can pace themselves. In other words, maybe it's not the boys who are flawed but our expectations of them.

It would be lovely if those of us with sons who have been labeled "hyperactive" could remake the world to suit them. But, for the moment, we have to adapt to this one. As such, the Ritalin solution is tempting, to say the least. But parents whose sons have behavior problems should exhaust other alternatives before turning to medication. . . .

In our own case . . . we decided to try to resist [Ritalin]. Instead, we have encouraged physical activity such as basketball and karate lessons, enrolled him in a camp to help develop his social skills, and talked often with his teachers. We try to give free rein to his artistic and musical talents, and encourage his uncanny ability to develop complicated strategies for winning our family marathons of Risk, Stratego, and Monopoly. Things around our house get pretty hectic at times, but so far, we've managed to keep him off medication.

Above all, says Armstrong, parents of active, energetic boys should trust their instincts. "Think hard about all you know about your son," he suggests, "and don't allow comments about his short attention span or high energy to be negative."[2]

There are many excellent teachers. Your child's reaction will vary from teacher to teacher. Pay attention to your child's feedback about a teacher. There may possibly be personality conflicts that will impede learning. We all have good days and bad days, but if your child repeatedly complains about a teacher or frets about school, get in the classroom and figure out the problem.

You can do this by volunteering. Your child may not even understand what is making her uncomfortable at school. Discussing it with the teacher will give you the teacher's version of the problem, but there is no better way to understand what is going on than by spending time in the classroom. I did this many times with my kids, and it is a very eye-opening experience. Sometimes it is not the teacher at all but the pressure your child is putting upon himself. It is impossible to fully understand the problems at school until you put yourself in the classroom and witness it firsthand.

I once had a teacher who did not want me in her classroom. I persisted until she let me correct papers in the back of the room. I knew my presence was needed when a child (not my own) came to me and thanked me for coming to help in the classroom. She said, "When you are here, our teacher treats us nice."

When problems arise in school, you can always listen to the advice of other parents. Some will have good information that may help you with a troubling situation. However, remember, every child is unique, especially yours, and the feedback you get from your child is always the best. If, after you spend time in the classroom, you can see that your child is struggling and doubt the environment will change, you need to make the change happen. Your child's motivation is too precious to ignore. Discuss the situation with the principal, and ask for a classroom change. A good principal will understand and be helpful in finding a solution. If you do not have the support of the principal, hold your ground. You have the right to request the best atmosphere of learning for your child. Remember, you are responsible to protect your child and his motivation. There is nothing more precious.

Change of Environment

Collin signed up for a calculus class during his junior year of high school. He was nervous about taking a tough class, but his current math teacher assured him he had done well in her class and he had the aptitude to be successful. During the first few weeks of the class, Collin struggled. He could not understand his new teacher's explanations. When he asked for help, his teacher suggested he give up and go to a lower math class. Collin felt like a failure. His father visited the school and met with Collin's math teacher. He was disappointed in this teacher's critique of Collin. He visited the counselor's office and gave her the information she needed to investigate. The counselor talked to Collin's past math teacher, checking his past grades and test scores. The counselor came to the conclusion that Collin should be able to succeed in this calculus class, especially since Collin was willing to try. She moved Collin to another teacher. Collin completed the class successfully.

Sometimes you must fall back on good common sense when it concerns your child's education. We often get caught up in trying to cram our kids' brains with excessive amounts of information. Too much pressure on a child will make her despise school. Children are children for such a short time period; please let them enjoy their childhood while they can. If you want to keep your children enthusiastic about learning, let them choose the pace.

Keep your child's education in perspective. We all know that grades and test scores are important, but sometimes, as parents, we put more importance on the grades than on what our kids are actually learning.

Education is not about memorizing and regurgitating the answers. It is about teaching a child to think and analyze. Simple changes will make big differences in your child's education. One of those changes can be a teacher. There are magical teachers who have the ability to "light a fire" under a child. Thomas Sowell wrote an editorial analyzing a criterion for good teachers.

> If your criterion for judging teachers is how much their students learn, then you can end up with a wholly different list of who are the best teachers. Some of the most unimpressive-looking teachers have consistently turned out students who know their subject far better than teachers

who cut a more dashing figure in the classroom and receive more lavish praise from their students or attention from the media.

My own experience as an undergraduate student at Harvard was completely consistent with what I learned as a teenager. One of my teachers—Professor Arthur Smithies—was a highly respected scholar but was widely regarded as a terrible teacher. Yet what he taught me has stayed with me for more than forty years, and his class determined the course of my future career. . . .

Smithies not only taught us particular things. He got us to think—often by questioning us in a way that forced us to follow out the logic of what we were saying to its ultimate conclusion. Often some policy that sounded wonderful, if you looked only at the immediate results, would turn out to be counterproductive if you followed your own logic beyond stage one.

In later years, I would realize that many disastrous policies had been created by thinking no further than stage one. Getting students to think systematically beyond stage one was a lifetime contribution to their understanding. . . .

Arthur Smithies would never get a teaching award by the standards of the education establishment today. But he rates a top award by a much older standard: By their fruits ye shall know them.[3]

Whenever I find myself pushing my kids too hard with their education, I read excerpts from Robert Fulghum's *All I Really Need to Know I Learned in Kindergarten.*

All I really need to know about how to live and what to do and how to be I learned in kindergarten. Wisdom was not at the top of the graduate-school mountain, but there in the sandpile at the Sunday School. These are the things I learned:

Share everything. Play fair. Don't hit people. Put things back where you found them. Clean up your own mess. Don't take things that aren't yours. Say you're sorry when you hurt somebody. Wash your hands before you eat. Flush. Warm cookies and cold milk are good for you. Live a balanced life—learn some and think some and draw and paint and sing and dance and play and work every day some.

Take a nap every afternoon. When you go out into the world, watch for traffic, hold hands, and stick together. Wonder. Remember the little seed in the Styrofoam cup: The roots go down and the plants go up and nobody really knows how or why, but we are all like that.

Goldfish and hamsters and white mice and even the little seed in the plastic cup—they all die. So do we. And then remember the Dick-and-Jane books and the first word you learned—the biggest word of all—LOOK.

Everything you need to know is there somewhere. The Golden Rule and love and basic sanitation. Ecology and politics and equality and sane living. . . .

Think what a better world it would be if we all—the whole world—had cookies and milk about three o'clock every afternoon and then lay down with our blankies for a nap. Or if all governments had as a basic policy to always put things back where they found them and clean up their own mess.

And it is still true, no matter how old you are—when you go out into the world, it is best to hold hands and stick together.[4]

Our school systems are not perfect. If you get involved and stay positive, your child can excel. Be careful when it comes to your child and his education. Protect his motivation, understand his learning patterns, and do not push too hard. If you nag him about doing his homework, you are removing the responsibility from him and heaping it upon your own shoulders. Instead, sit down with him and be willing to help. If you understand the workload your child carries, you will have better positioned yourself to assist. Learning can and should be exciting.

CHAPTER EIGHT

Teenagers

Not only are the teenage years a very puzzling time for you as a parent, but they are also very confusing for your child. At this time, many of the strange things your child will do might cause you to wonder if this child is the same one you gave birth to.

During these years, the best advice for parents to cope is to show large amounts of understanding and love to your teenager. It is important to remember that teenagers are going through enormous physical and psychological changes. Between the ages of seventeen and twenty-one, there is extensive maturation of the brain's frontal lobes. This process allows young people to think more abstractly, plan better for the future, and foresee the consequences of their actions. Keep in mind that this is a process, and each child will develop naturally at his own pace.

When our kids become teenagers, they take on the outward appearances of adults, yet they still lack adult experience, wisdom, and responsibility. You should not be too astounded when one minute your teenager shows the maturity of an adult and the next minute suddenly flips back into child mode, acting irresponsibly. They, too, are trying to understand and cope with the changes in their bodies, along with the accompanying social changes. I have found it best to think of kids at this age as mere adolescents encased in adult bodies. Their brains are still very childlike. Patience will become your greatest attribute as the parent of a teenager.

Physical Changes

While you work on teaching yourself patience, you might want to prepare your teenager for the changes she will go through. If you want her to listen to you, begin your explanations long before she hits the teenage years. It is good for children to know about the changes that accompany puberty before those changes happen. There are plenty of books on the subject, and reading them first will give you confidence in your presentation. It might be easiest to begin with a medical definition. However you do it, adapt your explanation to make your child feel comfortable. Each child must understand that everyone goes through this change. They are not alone in this experience.

Children need to understand the body and its functions. Explain the change in hormones and how this will affect them. Their body will grow faster now than at any other time of their life. Boys' shoulders will widen and their voices change. Girls' bodies will develop curves, and girls will experience new emotions.

As pre-teens begin to physically grow, they often become confused and forgetful. Patricia, a mother whose oldest son began his growth period after his thirteenth birthday, noticed that her son would sit in his room and stare at the walls for hours:

> I would walk by his room and observe, in amazement,
> that his lethargic body did not change its position or

expression. When I finally asked him what he was thinking about, he responded brilliantly, "I dunno."

This "I dunno" came from a child who, previous to
this growth spurt, had been very active. I truly believed
an alien was living in my son's body. My son grew six
inches in six months, and overnight had enough facial hair
to begin shaving. I wish I had been more prepared and
would have recognized the signs. I am pleased to report
that when this teenage developmental stage was over, my
son returned. He is now a very successful adult.

Puberty is unpredictable. Every child will go through puberty at different
times and react to it in different ways, but there are a few common traits.
School will become difficult, not because they have lost any intelligence, but
because the ability to focus or follow instructions may temporarily become
cloudy. Be prepared—grades may drop. Teens in puberty often become
moody, insecure, argumentative, and impulsive and have odd sleeping patterns. In this stage, I found that many teenagers want to sleep all the time,
except when they are eating. To help you understand the fog surrounding
your teenager, imagine she is in a permanent state of jet lag. The change in
your children will seem strange, so, once again, be patient, and let your children know that you love them.

Friends Are Important

As a parent, you need to acknowledge that a peer group is very important to
a teenager. Growing up is much easier if your child has friends to commis-
erate with. The time spent with friends away from family will bring a change
in your child's perspective and attitude. During this time, it is important to
remember that you are still a powerful confidant and teacher. Your child
may not appear to listen to anything you say, but he does hear more than
he lets on.

Dr. Lawrence Kutner, chair of the Peer Pressure Smoking/Advisory Board at Harvard Medical School, reminds us how influential peer pressure is during the teen years.

> At the high school I attended in the 1960s, 12th graders could relax in the "Senior Lounge." It was the only place in the school where students could smoke, and it reeked of tobacco. Some of the seniors who went there started the habit because their friends did it, and because they saw smoking as a sign of maturity.
>
> I stayed away from the lounge and its smoke. My mother, a lifelong smoker, was dying of cancer that was probably caused by her addiction.
>
> That lounge is long gone. We know much more about the dangers of smoking. But the peer pressure that led some of my classmates to start smoking is still there. Teenagers increasingly look to their friends for feed-back on how they're coming across and what they might change. I see this in my son and remember it from my own adolescence.
>
> Peer pressure is one reason why adolescents are at much greater risk than adults for starting to smoke. It's also why it's so important for parents to take an active and repeated stand against smoking. Parents know their children best. But sometimes we all need some guidance on when and how to talk about tough topics.
>
> Kids today feel social pressure in countless ways, from clothing and music choices to risky areas such as drugs, sex, and smoking. The intensity of peer pressure varies from situation to situation. Adolescents experience it when friends or others they admire pressure them to do something they don't want to do, or when they feel they

have to do something to fit in.

Kids say peer pressure makes them feel they're being pulled in two directions. They may not want to do what they're feeling pressured to do, but they're also afraid of losing their friends if they say no. Kids worry about being on people's bad sides and really want to avoid feeling like outsiders.

During adolescence, kids assert their independence and explore their identity. Dr. Jacqueline Lerner, a professor of psychology at Boston College, says, 'Adolescents behave in accordance with their perceptions which do not always match reality.' You can help them accurately perceive the world by sharing your experiences and a more factual perspective on reality. Your words do make a difference, even if it seems your kids aren't paying attention.[1]

Peers and pop culture will influence your child's choice of clothing, hairstyles, music, and even personality. That's OK. You might not like her music or the way she looks, but if you will accept these relatively minor choices, she will be more likely to listen to you on bigger decisions that really matter.

C. Ross Clement, a licensed clinical social worker, teaches ways to enhance the chance that our children will respond positively.

Ironically, the time when children can benefit most from their parents' wisdom is often the time when they are least likely to accept it. Adolescent children, in particular, strive to become independent, and the urgency of that drive, heightened by the pull of peers and worldly influence, sometimes draws them away from those who could help them the most. Sadly, their parents, wanting desperately to help, sometimes watch helplessly as they make unfortunate mistakes. Headstrong children, bent on doing things their own way, rebuff the most loving of fathers and mothers.

As parents, how can we keep the doors of communication open? . . .

Communication includes every thought, feeling, act, or desire that is shared verbally and nonverbally between parents and children. It is impossible not to communicate. . . .

Sometimes a change of heart is needed before good communication is possible. Some parents drive their children away through lecturing, moralizing, interrogating, judging, condemning, threatening, blaming, criticizing, and ridiculing. . . .

Changes of the heart are reflected in the countenance and in the way we talk and listen to each other. . . .

As parents, the single most important thing we can do for our children is to love them . . . When our children know that we truly love them, they are more likely to listen to our counsel, follow our example, and accept our discipline.

Without love, a parent's expression of disappointment can be perceived as rejection and, oft repeated, can damage the child's sense of worth. . . . Family life without love is empty and unhappy.

Learn and use good communication skills. . . . A few of these skills include:

- Showing nonverbal interest in what your child has to say by paying attention, maintaining eye contact without staring, and appearing interested instead of distant or bothered.
- Asking questions that invite your child to talk, such as, "It looks like something is troubling you. Want to

tell me about it?"

- Selectively rephrasing what you hear, such as, "You're worried that others don't like you." Rephrasing conveys interest in and understanding of your child's message. If you didn't hear it accurately, your child can clarify the message.

Listening is particularly challenging when your child is upset with you. Most parents want their children's approval and feel threatened, defensive, or rejected when criticized. However, a listening ear has healed many troubled relationships. Instead of reacting to your child's anger, try listening, instead, without defending yourself. If your child is critical of you, acknowledge if there is truth in what he or she says. A child's angry feelings often subside when listening occurs. . . . By honestly admitting an error, you will take a major step toward rebuilding a trusting relationship with your child. . . .

Start responding to your children's feelings when they are very young. If you wait until they are older, they . . . may not share their feelings with you. However, it is never too late to enhance your communication skills. . . .

Sometimes behavioral changes do not come until the child is convinced that our course corrections are more than fleeting bursts of energy. Consequently, we must persist in our efforts, even when our children do not respond immediately. As [you become] more . . . loving and skillful in [your] interactions . . . [your child will] rejoin his family socially, emotionally, and spiritually.[2]

Your influence is real. Put yourself in the best position to help guide your child as he struggles with peer pressure, examines his options, and gradually becomes a mature, independent thinker.

Why, at this age, are our children so vulnerable? Think back, and you may remember the excitement of moving out of grade school and on to middle school or high school. Can you recall the uncomfortable details, such as how it feels to walk into a high school cafeteria and have everyone scrutinize your words, your walk, your clothes, your entire worth? Kids can be overwhelmed and intimidated by the new surroundings, the new faces, and their sudden fall in stature from being the oldest in the school to the youngest. To fit in, they will experience pressure to try things they know are not right.

As they develop, adolescents often struggle to understand how others, especially their peers, view them. Reassure your child that while friends will sometimes pressure him to join in the activities of the group, a true friend will respect his choices. The most important concept for your child to grasp is that he needs to make his own decisions. This will not be difficult for the child who has been given the opportunity to freely express himself at home in a Safe Haven. If he has gained self-confidence early on in life, he will not be swayed to join in when friends make unwise choices.

If you, as a parent, have included your child in family decisions, this process will be easy, but if you have dictated rules and instructions to your child most of her life, she will struggle making decisions independent of her friends.

Promote independent thinking. Praise your child when he makes decisions on his own. Encourage your child to be a leader, to form opinions, and to make decisions based on his own judgment. Ask questions about incidents that occur in their lives: why things happen and the consequences of certain actions. Talk with your teen. When you ask questions, do not criticize the responses: "Why do you think your friends are doing these things?" "What do you think of their choices?"

Having your child think through these problems can be just as important as the answers. The more your children learn to trust in themselves and their own abilities to make independent decisions, the less vulnerable your children will be to peer pressure.

Know your child's friends. Make sure her friends feel welcome in your home. If they feel comfortable, they will spend more time at your home and less time in unsupervised places. Do not be disapproving of your child's choice of friends. If one of your daughter's friends smokes, tell your daughter you disapprove of the smoking. Do not say, "I don't like your friend." If you focus on the behavior, your child will be more likely to discuss a friend's flaws and not be defensive that you are attacking your child's choice in friends.

Some kids take inappropriate risks because they're bored, so get them involved. Keeping your children busy in groups or clubs that fit their interests can reduce the chances of boredom and will provide your children with a new set of strengths. When they find something they like to do or talents they have, their self-esteem skyrockets. Teenagers who feel good about themselves are less likely to join the irrational behavior of their peer group.

We have discussed some of the problems that occur when a child has a strong peer group, but what do you do when your child struggles to fit in or find friends? In her article on cliques, Betsy Rubiner explains how you can help your child:

> Girls engage in catty behavior and nasty comments, judging each other on appearance and material possessions. Boys' cliques behave similarly, but emphasis is more likely to be placed on athletic ability, physical prowess, and appearance. These groups can seem all-important in the lives of kids seeking to define themselves and longing to bolster their sense of self-confidence. To be in a group makes kids feel safe, that they belong. The irony is that groups can be a huge support and a way to survive adolescence. But they can have a destructive influence, too . . .
>
> When a member of the clique is taunting another student, fellow members are expected to join in, or at least stand by and do nothing. "This teaches moral cowardice," says Wiseman. "In the face of injustice or cruelty

being done to you or others, you look the other way. Or you rationalize it as the price you have to pay so you'll be accepted. No one wants to be left out." One suburban mom, Gina Kurban stated it this way, "It's very difficult to see your child in pain and not know how to fix it." Especially when children aren't forthcoming about details.

But at some point, every child is bound to experience some sense of being excluded or even unpopular. Such situations seldom have a quick-fix solution and perhaps that's just as well. If there's a silver lining to these experiences, it's that kids can use them to develop a greater sense of self-reliance and learn how to remind themselves of their good qualities. Here are some ways parents can help.

Get the lay of the land. To find out your child's situation, have him draw a map of where kids sit in the cafeteria or play on the playground. . . . Encourage him to talk about the social situation and pay attention to all the key players in this real-life soap opera. And like a soap opera, you should expect to go through several episodes before anything gets resolved.

Avoid knee-jerk responses. Wait three or four days for the kids to work it through themselves. If your child is being bullied or physically threatened, don't wait for things to get out of hand. Talk to teachers and school officials.

Let your child lead. Instead of telling your child what you think the problem is, help her examine her situation.

"Offer constructive suggestions. To ease rejection or isolation, help your child find new activities and people—the more she sees herself in different ways, the more she's able to bounce back," says Wiseman.

> Parents can turn the unpleasant situation into a learn-
> ing experience, using it as a chance to remind a child that
> how she felt can help shape how she'll treat others. That
> in turn will ultimately make her a stronger, more under-
> standing person.[3]

Teenagers want and need the support of their parents, yet, at the same time, they distance themselves from you. They need room to grow and change, but they also need you to stay involved and close to them. This is the time of life when they begin gaining a sense of autonomy. They need to find where they fit in the world, and it is very important for them to feel they matter. Teenagers want to belong to their families and a peer group. Your teen is trying to shape who he will become, so every interaction he has affects his opinions of life.

With this sense of autonomy comes the challenge of having your child pull away from you and possibly your beliefs. It is hard to be challenged, especially by your own child. Teenagers may be curt in their remarks, disrespectfully saying things that are hurtful and shocking, but let them challenge. Much of what they are saying is not really what they believe. They are only trying on a variety of opinions, as they would sport a new stylish outfit. They want to see how the fit feels. Laugh with them, joke with them, but gently remind them of where you stand and what you believe. This can be done in a loving way without belittling or making them feel as though their opinions do not matter.

As your child goes through this change, it can be very frightening for you as a parent. It is a fear of the unknown. Many parents get stuck in this stage and parent out of fear: fear of drugs and alcohol, fear of teenage sex—basi-cally a fear of losing their children. The definition of parenting out of fear depicts people afraid of what they do not understand. When you can admit to yourself that you don't understand what is going on with your teen, that you need help, it is then that you are open to learning. A humble parent never fails. The greatest quality you can have as a parent is to be humble, which means to be teachable.

Continue to educate yourself. Go to the library, read books, take classes, meditate, and observe others. Your child has a lot to teach you, so be watching and listening for it. Learn and be open to what you can change. With a humble attitude, you will find yourself able to love this teenager no matter what she presents to you. If you let them, the teenage years can be the most rewarding years you spend with your child.

CHAPTER NINE

Teaching Your Child

How do you teach children? As parents, we understand the importance of teaching our children values such as honesty, compassion, dedication, and personal worthiness. We also know our children need to learn practical tasks like mowing the lawn, budgeting money, cleaning bedrooms, and maintaining personal hygiene, along with many others. It is not difficult to give instructions and even demand our kids do what we say. When our kids have tasks they need to accomplish, or should I say tasks we need them to accomplish, it does not have to be a negative experience. So how do you go about teaching so many correct principles in a positive way?

There is a never-ending list of items we *should* be teaching our children. As parents, we begin with the best intentions, but failure can seem amazingly imminent when our children react negatively to our methods. The problem is not in our desire. The problem lies in our technique. If you are teaching the way your parents taught and that never worked, it should not come as a surprise if you are failing.

Teaching by Example

Teaching by example has been touched upon in previous chapters. We need to continually be reminded that teaching by example is the way children learn most of what they know. As parents, everything you do is absorbed by your child. Teaching by example can be likened to osmosis. Osmosis is a gradual, often unconscious absorption of knowledge gained through continual exposure. Your child is always watching you, so you are always teaching by example.

How are we doing as parents? Maria Cortex gives us an idea:

> The results of Public Agenda's recent national survey tells us that 61 percent of American parents rate their generation as "fair" or "poor" at raising children.
>
> The survey of 1,607 parents of school-age children found big gaps between parents' efforts to teach good values and their perceived success in doing so. More than half of the parents surveyed said they believe they are doing a worse job of parenting than their own parents did. . . . [T]oday's parents need to consider how different the world is now than when they were children. . . . Use of illegal drugs became more prevalent and the youths of the country drifted from their parents' bedrock ideals as never before. . . . Probably the biggest difference between today's parents and their parents is technology and affluence. . . . If parents want their children to have good values, they must model good values. If they want their children to be charitable, they themselves must give to others. If they believe honesty is an important trait, they have to be truthful in

their dealings with their children. If a religious upbringing is important to parents, they have to put forth the effort to get the kids (and themselves) to worship services and work hard to live by the precepts of their particular faith.[1]

Improving your own life will be the best way to teach by example. Teaching by example is the most powerful tool available. However, it may not be so much about what you teach as about when and how you teach it.

Teaching through Mistakes

When a child makes a mistake or has an error in judgment, it is time to teach a worthwhile lesson. Thomas Edison said, "Don't call it a failure. Call it an education." A mistake provides you with a golden opportunity to teach. Most of us hate it when our children make mistakes. When a mistake is made, we rarely think, "What a great opportunity this is for me. I now have the opportunity to teach!"

A child's mistake can be embarrassing, especially when the mistake occurs in front of a large group of people. It can be especially humiliating if you know the people. Please try not to be concerned with what others will think. Focus on your child and what will help him the most.

When teaching through mistakes, concentrate on timing and how you will teach. Never, ever, ever correct your child in front of people. It is also a "no-no" to correct them smack-dab in the middle of the mistake. Give your child the opportunity to realize, on her own, what she has done wrong. Then, in a calmer moment or at a later time, discuss it. Do not allow yourself to accuse or demean your children in anyway.

To begin, you could ask how it made them feel, or how they would change the situation if they could do it again. They may need your help understanding how to solve the problem. Your goal is to talk it through with your children, helping them realize what went wrong, not to punish them. When you humiliate children, you have robbed yourself of the opportunity to teach.

They will no longer listen to you. The way you handle difficult situations with your kids makes a difference in what you will be able to teach them. Your goal as a parent is to help your children learn from their own experiences in positive ways.

Let me explain with a tender story from Yoshihiko Kikuchi entitled *Broken Windows, Broken Hearts*.

> As a young boy playing baseball with my friends, I hit the ball over the playground fence and broke the neighbor's large glass window. The last few times the ball had gone over the fence, we were told to be careful. But I was not careful. Frightened, we all ran away.
>
> In the evening, I felt so bad that I told my mother what had happened. My mother was a widow, and we were very poor at the time. But she said that I must go to the neighbor and apologize. And she said, "Here is the money you must take."
>
> I was afraid to go by myself, so my mother said, "I will come with you." She apologized to the neighbor and paid the money for me. During the next few months, I earned small amounts every week and finally paid back what I owed my mother.
>
> I learned a great lesson from my mother. The thing I did wrong must be apologized for and must be paid for. But at that time, I couldn't afford to pay. So my mother sacrificed to pay on my behalf. If my mother had not helped me and insisted that I apologize, my feelings of guilt and shame would have stayed with me for a long time. And I could never have faced my neighbor again.[2]

As a wise mother, Mrs. Kikuchi knew what needed to be done to help her son learn from his mistake. She knew her son did not have enough money to pay for the window. She also realized that her young son was frightened and not yet mature enough to go alone to apologize for the broken window. Anger might have prevailed, but Yoshihiko knew he had made a mistake. An angry reaction from his mother would only have degraded him more, leaving shame and guilt as his lesson. Instead, she handled the situation with love and understanding. The mistake became a great teaching moment that will stay with Mr. Kikuchi for the rest of his life. *A mistake is never a mistake if something is learned from it.*

Teaching Bit by Bit

When a child is not grasping what you are trying to teach, could it be that what you are trying to teach is too overwhelming for the child? Break tasks into small pieces. No one likes to fail, so children often react by doing nothing. Judi Light Hopson, Emma H. Hopson, and Ted Hagen give a great example of how to effectively teach kids how to help with household chores by breaking it down:

> Is your family fighting a lot over household chores? Is
> there a daily tug-of-war over laundry, vacuuming, and
> picking up clutter? If nothing's working, consider that
> humans aren't instinctively good at such jobs. They need
> training. Your kids and spouse watching you do chores
> doesn't count as "training." Human beings do not learn the
> art of tidying or cleaning by osmosis. . . . The human brain
> must be able to visualize the specifics of a certain task
> in order to complete it. Even a mundane chore, such as
> sweeping the kitchen, requires a set of skills. Think about
> it. Sweeping involves breaking the floor into manageable squares, sweeping up little piles of dirt and making
> those little piles travel onto the dust pan. Teenagers

don't automatically know how to sweep a large room or organize a pile of junk. Small children don't necessarily perceive how to put away toys. . . .

These tips can help you train those brains:

- Break chores down into 10-minute tasks. Label tasks such as cleaning a sink, sweeping the kitchen, or vacuuming one room as a 10-minute chore.

- Assign every family member one 10-minute chore each day. Put a detailed list on the refrigerator beside each person's name. Do this until your spouse and kids see how teamwork adds up. For example, four people working 40 minutes per day, tallies up to 20 hours per month. . . .

While children can be sharp intellectually, they are not necessarily wise in matters of judgment and assessment. For instance, children can't perceive how to properly sort dirty laundry. . . . Coach them until they can easily put the reds, whites, darks and "delicates" into separate piles.

"I decided last year to train my family to do chores," says a mother we'll call Debbie. "At first," she explains, "I kept everyone on the same tasks for two weeks. Then, I added more tasks and started rotating what they did." Debbie says that her children and her husband were slow learners. But, they finally got the hang of how to master sweeping, cleaning, and breaking large tasks into doable chunks.

If you think your children's lack of help on chores is stressful to you now, wait until they marry. Their failure to keep up household chores can cause huge rifts in their relationships.[3]

Parents, never drive your children but lead them along, giving them knowledge as their minds are able to understand. Lead them, guide them, and be by their side when they need help.

Teaching Using Guided Practice

An important principle to use when teaching children is guided practice. Guided practice is a gentle version of teaching your child to correctly do what you want. *Parents who succeed with troubled children teach the child what they want as opposed to just teaching what they don't want.* When trying to teach children what you want them to do, create a plan.

Say you want to teach your child how to clean the bathroom. Begin by walking your daughter through the process step by step, showing her how to clean the toilet, countertops, mirrors, and shower. With simple and easy directions, it does not seem too difficult for her to handle. However, the first time she does the task on her own, you wonder what planet she was on during your initial demonstration. There are streaks on the mirror, stains around the toilet, and dirt on the floor. The natural response of most adults is to find the child, drag them into the bathroom and point out every mistake and make them redo the bathroom. Before you ruin the teaching moment, let's try another approach. Keep in mind that your child may have finished her task thinking she has done a good job.

No matter how poor a job, begin by thanking her for cleaning the bathroom. This will be difficult to say the words, but remember, your child has no idea you are not pleased with her attempt to clean the bathroom. Say nothing else. Then choose another moment in time when you are both in the bathroom together say, "Oh look, this mirror has a streak on it. It is tough to clean a mirror and not leave streaks."

Then clean the streaks from the mirror, explaining the process again, with her watching. You have just helped your child take note of something she normally would never have observed. Additionally, you have done it in a way that does not attack her cleaning ability. If you criticize a child for something she has done, especially something she did not want to do in the first place, you have shot yourself in the foot. You will never get her to do it again. She will make sure to do a terrible job on every task assigned so that you will never ask for her help again. It is a good idea to refrain from having this conversation or correcting her when she is tired, stressed, or in a bad mood.

Children do not need discipline or punishment to learn. They do need explanations. Wouldn't it be more productive to spend your time coming up with creative ways to teach a new concept? Many of us spend far too much time thinking up new ways to discipline.

How do your kids respond when you set more rules? When you nag a child over and over about accomplishing a chore, does it work? As we have talked about many times in this book, harping on a child over responsibilities kills any motivation to get the job done. If you can get in the habit of speaking softly and stating things only once, you will be amazed how well your child will hear you and understand with crystal clarity.

To stop the nagging, here are some practical solutions to try. As a parent, allow yourself to pick only three improvements for your child within an allotted time period. To give you an idea, here are some possibilities:

1. Brush teeth after every meal.

2. Pick the clothes up off their bedroom floor.

3. Get homework done when it is due.

Note that it will be easier if you decide upon the three tasks with your child. Be specific and, as discussed previously, break the task into pieces. Let your child be responsible for the job. Try not to impose your personal time limits to get the chores done but, rather, guidelines of getting the chore accomplished weekly or maybe twice a month (unless, of course, it's a personal hygiene issue).

Let's start with the teeth. Take the time to explain why it is important to brush your teeth after every meal. Discuss tooth decay and bad breath.

Children, and even teenagers, may not understand the results of not brushing. To really gross them out, show a few pictures of tooth decay. Take it as far as you need to with your child. When your child understands the concept of brushing teeth, it will become automatic, and you will be released from continually reminding him of this responsibility.

When it comes to cleaning a bedroom, another discussion on why keeping the floor picked up is necessary. Show them how much nicer their clothes look when put on a hanger. You might want to explain how that 'really cool t-shirt' will last longer if it is not consistently trampled while lying on the floor. It also doesn't hurt to remind them that clothes strung across the floor for long periods of time become homes for spiders and bugs. Humor can and should be used in all suggestions to keep it positive.

This is a tough issue for teenagers, and sometimes the only solution to motivate is to spend time with them in their rooms talking and hanging up clothes. By doing this, you have discovered a great way to spend time together. Find out what is going on in their lives. Through the process, you are reminding them (without nagging) of how nice it is to reside in an organized environment.

Your third improvement will be based on the benefits of doing homework. Doing your homework results in good grades, which assists in getting into a good college. A good education provides a good job, which then gives financial freedom, allowing her to live life in the style she chooses. Site examples of individuals admired for successful academic achievements. Then, be by her side to help her study.

Do not expect perfection right away. It may take years to get the homework done on time or the clothes off the floor. The concept of hanging clothes on hangers may not become reality until they go away to college. Be patient. Eventually you will see improvement.

Over time, and as your child grows and changes, feel free to adapt the list of improvement choices. The idea is to keep your list to only three improvements at a time. You are teaching your child how to improve behaviors the two of you feel are important. If you can be patient with your child while she is learning, she will be patient with you as you learn how to teach without nagging.

This three-item rule helps to maintain the Safe Haven, but it will only work if you have stopped pestering your child. If you can stop the nagging, you will produce a child who is loaded with self-esteem, one who will eventually understand and live by the concepts you are teaching. It is hard to do, and it requires zipping your mouth shut when you want to say something negative. To accomplish your quest to quit nagging, you may have to put your spouse on guard to stop you, but this is important, so do it! Think of it this way: when you nag, you take the responsibility from your child's shoulders and stack it upon your own. When a child is allowed to be responsible, even when he makes a mistake, he will learn—especially if it results in tooth decay!

If you try this—teaching by example using guided practice, choosing the right moment to assist, and breaking tasks into pieces—you will quickly begin to see small successes while teaching your children. Don't expect big things to happen. Be grateful for the small things because small things add up to big things later.

Teaching Your Child about Sex

Sex is a hard topic for most parents to discuss with their children. The subject of sexuality in today's world is presented openly on such a constant basis that your kids usually know more than you think. No matter what the level of education, it is important to have regular discussions with your children about sex. If you want your child to have correct information, you need to be the one doing the teaching, not their friends.

Your home is the place where they should learn correct principles. It is important for three things to be expressed and understood by your child:

1. We are responsible for our behavior and for our own happiness.

2. The improper use of sex can create great misery and unhappiness.

3. The sexual drive is strong and healthy and was meant to be enjoyed in a mature relationship.

When you are teaching human sexuality to your children, be honest and accurate. Dr. Phil has good advice on the subject:

- Define sex with your child. . . . [I]f it involves a sex organ, it's sex.
- Talk to your child about sex . . . early and often.
- Monitor "the four W's": who, what, when, and where.
- Give them correct information.
- Educate your child about the health risks.
- Make your child aware of the long-term effects on his/her reputation and self-esteem.
- As a parent, you must make your child feel special.[4]

When you discuss the topic of sex, tell your children exactly what you believe. The code of morality presented by society will only confuse your child. Children need help figuring out what will make them happy. Teen sex is not the answer. Erma Bombeck puts it into perspective. A local YMCA was discussing incorporating a class teaching infants how to swim. Apparently, babies can hold their breath and even float at three months of age. The head of the department acknowledged babies can float but they need more than instincts to swim; they need the maturity and intelligence to get out of the pool. A baby who decided to take a swim without an adult would drown from exhaustion. Bombeck saw a correlation. She said:

> To me, that analogy applies to fifteen-year-olds having sex. They can do it. It's instinctive and doesn't demand a lot of skill. But they may pay the ultimate price for not having the wisdom or the judgment to save themselves.
>
> So, what's the big deal? Why don't parents want their kids to have a good time? Young people know about the risks. Besides, all the other kids are doing it.

There isn't a person in the world who will admit (if he is honest) that he is the same person after his first sexual experience that he was before. He left something behind that was so special even he didn't realize it. Some call it innocence. I'm not sure it has a name. But whatever it is, it's impossible to recapture it again. Even if you are married, the relationship changes.

Age knows what youth has not yet learned—that there is time. There are patches of life that follow a pattern of growth. There's a time for discovery, a time for adventure, a time to be a child, a time to learn, a time to find your place. Don't ever try to fast-forward it. Enjoy every minute. You get only one chance to be fifteen.

I watched a mother on Oprah's show one morning brag about how hip she was that she encouraged her two young teenage daughters to bring their boyfriends home and sleep with them in their own beds on clean sheets. She was pleased they were popular. (I bet they were.)

It brought back a picture of little babies learning how to swim. They get a lot of media attention, but heaven help the babies who thought they were swimming when in fact they were only trying to emulate adults.[5]

Let your kids be kids. Teach them that for everything there is a season and that there is no hurry to rush into sex. Talk to your children about sex often. Tell them to delay sex until they are older and more mature. Teenagers are not prepared to handle the emotional ties that come with sexual intercourse. Moms and Dads, they need to hear this from you.

Joseph Plambeck with the Knight Ridder/Tribune News Service gives us the research we need in his article, "Teens with Closer Ties to Moms Tend to Delay Having Sex."

Teenagers who have close relationships with their mothers wait longer to begin having sex, according to an extensive study of American adolescents reported Wednesday.

But researchers also concluded the relationship must go beyond simply telling teens to abstain from sex or warning them about the dangers.

Mothers need to clearly communicate their own values and also know their teenager's friends and the parents of their friends if they want to delay teen sex, the study found.

"We need to be tuned in to what's happening in our children's lives," said Dr. Robert Blum, director of the University of Minnesota's Center for Adolescent Health and Development and the study's author. The new report is drawn from two studies based on a large survey of teens and their parents. . . .

Last year, the Centers for Disease Control and Prevention reported that 46 percent of high school students had had sexual intercourse at some point. The disease control agency also reported that 42 percent of sexually active high school students had not used a condom in their last sexual encounter.

The new study found that even mothers who talk with their teens frequently are largely unaware of sexual activity. Only half of the mothers knew that their children were having sex, researchers said.

Often, the message of disapproving mothers becomes confused, the study found. Even when mothers strongly disapprove of their children having sex, 30 percent of girls and nearly 45 percent of boys don't know their mothers' views.

The study found that girls whose mothers have college degrees are less likely to become sexually active. But teens with mothers who are highly religious are no less likely than their peers to have sex.[6]

When it comes to teaching your kids about sex, talk a lot. Before any prom date or weekend spent hanging out in mixed company, talk with your son or daughter about sex. It doesn't have to be a long, drawn-out, difficult conversation. You can bring humor into the conversation. Your goal is to remind them of who they are and what they stand for. Finally, as always, remember: *children don't care how much you know until they know how much you care.*

CHAPTER TEN

Thou Shalt Not Judge

"I like you just the way you are."

That famous quote came from children's television personality, Mr. Rogers. Mr. Rogers based his television show on the fact that if somebody cares about you, you will care about others.

When you look at your child, is it possible to overlook her flaws and love her just the way she is? As parents, we spend much of our parenting time teaching and improving when what our children need the most is our approval and love. I printed and hung a quote on my refrigerator that jolts me back into reality whenever a wave of disapproval about my children or my children's friends begins to encompass me. It says:

Wouldn't it be nice if we looked at people and jelly beans

and we liked them all? And we didn't just choose the
people that we thought were pretty or smart, or ate just
the red or black jelly beans because they were our favorite
flavors, but realized that people and jelly beans come in a
variety and we can enjoy something about each one and
love them for what they are?

We have previously discussed how important it is to help children set
goals and succeed. Once they do set their goals, be cautious about putting
too much pressure on your kids to excel. Parents do their children no favors
by expecting too much. We all want what is best for our kids. William
Stixrud, a clinical neurologist who specializes in learning disorders, was
quoted saying:

> "I see a lot of parents who are chronically disappointed in
> their kids," Stixrud said. "When I ask them what would
> happen if they gave their kid the permission to be who he
> really is, many say they feel obligated to be disapproving or
> the kid will never make it in the world, be able to support
> himself, or get married. . . . The qualities needed to be a
> top student often are not the ones that bring success in the
> real world. . . . Many of those who make it big don't think
> like that. They pursue their own interests and set their
> own goals. They are risk takers."[1]

As parents, we are setting our kids up for failure and ourselves up for
disappointments when our expectations are too high. There is a line we must
never cross as parents; support your children, but do not take over, do not
push them, and let them motivate themselves. They are capable of setting
their own goals. When they actually choose their own goals, prepare yourself
to witness achievement, happiness, and, most importantly, your child discovering her drive to succeed.

Setting My Own Standards

Will was an excellent student. He worked hard for his grades, and it paid off. As a junior in high school, he had a strong GPA of 3.7. Will needed to do well on his SAT to be accepted into USC. He had already taken the SAT twice, but his scores were not high enough for him to be accepted. Will's mom had signed him up for multiple SAT prep courses. On this his third try, he felt prepared to do well on the test. When the test was over, Will was sure he would get a high score. Three weeks later his test scores arrived in the mail. Will found his scores were only a few points higher, still not high enough to be accepted into USC. Will's mother pushed Will to keep trying. Will was discouraged, and he was tired of taking tests. He decided to talk with his counselor about his options. Mr. Harris, Will's counselor, told Will he could take the SAT once more in order to get his scores submitted on time. He also presented Will with an alternative. He could attend a community college with a scholarship, get his associate's degree, and then transfer to his dream school, USC. Mr. Harris told Will not to discount the community college. They offered smaller classes with more personalized attention. Will took the SAT one more time to please his mother but could not raise his test scores. He finally went to the community college. While there, Will got involved in student government and wrote for the school paper. He quit putting so much pressure on himself and found he enjoyed his schoolwork. Two years later, when he graduated with his associate's degree, not only was he accepted to USC, but they also offered Will a journalism scholarship.

Too often we judge our kids on academics—SAT scores or admissions to prestigious colleges. When you do this, you are letting the world set the standards by which you judge your child. Be careful with this process. It is too easy to lose sight of who your child really is and what makes him happy.

Marianne M. Jennings, a professor at Arizona State University, wrote a column for the *Arizona Republic* on the benefits of raising plain old average kids. This article is titled, "Having Average Kids Isn't Such a Bad Thing."

When I had my first child, I had visions of a Rhodes scholar. By the time I had my third child, I was to the point of hoping they would have only misdemeanor convictions. Now that I have four children, I only pray that they don't commit the types of crimes that make the national news. . . .

I enrolled my oldest daughter in dance lessons when she was three. Right at the dinner hour, three nights each week, I rushed her to a studio where she made dance-like movements for an hour with a line of fifteen tiny mopheads. She would whine when we got her dressed for dance. "You could be another Paula Abdul," I used to assure her as I used a curling iron and White Rain stiff mist to get the requisite curls in place. And when she stepped out of the studio, she would look up at me with sad eyes that said, "Why are you doing this to me? It was childbirth, wasn't it? You're getting back at me."

Now that she is a teenager and I know her, her strengths, and what she enjoys and is good at doing, it's embarrassing to me that I forced her to tap away for the three months I could tolerate those pathetic post-Good-Ship-Lollipop humiliated eyes. This is where the parents of average children show their wisdom. Their children are free to explore and excel as they wish. There are no forced lessons. No contrived lifestyles. No parent of an average child is living vicariously through his or her child. Parents of average children have an odd inner strength that gives their children childhoods. . . .

Today, my children found a lizard and rescued it from the cat. . . . They want to make some popcorn tonight and watch "The Munsters" reruns. It's not headline stuff. It's a childhood. They're so average. I couldn't be more proud.[2]

Relax, be yourself, and have fun with your children. Fun is a necessity when raising children. You don't stop laughing because you grow old—you grow old because you stop laughing.

Gordon B. Hinckley, a prominent religious leader, said, "We've got to have a little humor in our lives. You had better take seriously that which should be taken seriously but, at the same time, we can bring in a touch of humor now and again. If the time ever comes when we can't smile at ourselves, it will be a sad time."[3]

Often, our children do not feel our approval because we become so involved with the day-to-day happenings of our lives that we forget to share our thoughts and feelings. It is important to strive to have reassuring relationships with our children. Children need to tell of their successes, and they also need to feel the comfort of telling their failures to a sympathetic listener. From you, they need to hear of your life experiences and understand your values. If you share with them the goals you have for the family, they will better understand why you act as you do. They will also better understand the decisions you make. Your children will understand your intentions and correctly interpret your actions. They will feel your love and not your condemnation.

As we end this section on judging and acceptance, remember one simple thing: know your children and their capabilities. You will then know what to expect of them. Do not compare them to siblings or friends, and never require more of them than they can give.

CHAPTER ELEVEN

Just Be Yourself

We are each born with a unique way of looking at the world. Children, in particular, have an unlimited potential for creative thought. Unfortunately, as kids grow up, much of their creativity is stifled in order to conform. It is a parent's role to help children discover that creativity. If you have successfully taken that first step and created a Safe Haven, you will be able to help your child begin this process. With the Safe Haven in place, you have established an environment where creativity can emerge naturally.

Helping your child discover their creativity should be fun. Being motivated and interested in learning are key elements for children. Creativity begins naturally in a child and develops as we age into adulthood.

To help, begin by appealing to your child's creativity through their senses: "Look over here!" "Taste this!" "Listen to that!"

Activities involving senses are excellent, yet simple methods to teach children about themselves and the world. Introducing your children to nature, new cultures, animals, museums, sports, or science provides endless possibilities for them to wrap their young brains around.

It is important that your children have the time to be creative. Creativity tends to flourish on days when children are not under pressure. Children need the time to explore ideas rather than constantly being saddled with too many after-school activities and the stress of growing up. Although it may drive a parent crazy, moments of doing nothing are essential for creativity, productivity, and peace of mind. Give your child the freedom and the space to daydream and explore.

Once you have found something that interests your children, assisting them to be creative is nothing more than becoming a cheerleader. One of the advantages we have as adults is that we see the relevance of what we are learning. The desire to learn or create will be stronger in children if you can put into perspective what they are creating. Make sure you support them, direct them, and cheer them along their chosen path. Jo Ann Larsen, DSW, describes it this way: "In life we are, in a sense, gardeners of our own selves, needing to transfer those selves from smaller to larger pots to get new growth and better blooms; and needing to strive toward maturity as the crises of our lives open up new opportunities for change."[1]

It is important to believe that every human being has been gifted with talents. Discovering these talents can be the difficult part, and it is our job as parents to help our children dig deep and find where they excel. Some children find their passions early, but for the majority of children, it will take years. Many of us as adults are just now discovering where we excel.

If a child is able to cultivate a passion early, it will bring excitement into her life. When a child discovers a gift that lies within, she is better equipped to battle with low self-esteem, drug abuse, or other problems that frustrate parents.

If you can give your child just a small taste of being good at something, he will want that feeling again and again. With the success of each accomplishment, children are far more excited to try new things. Small moments of success go a long way in motivating a child. Just as the ancient Chinese proverb says, "Give someone a fish and they eat for a day; teach someone to fish and they eat for a lifetime."

There are many ways to motivate your children to find their passions, so make sure your methods are not destructive. Be careful how you help. When you help, make sure you are not taking away your child's opportunity to discover. A child who is handed success is not learning the process, nor will she appreciate the results if she has not had a part in the search.

Many parents buy their children stuff, hoping it will help them find their talents. How often have you seen a child join a sports team decked out with the most expensive gear? Does that really help the child find his passion? What about when a parent signs up to coach an athletic team to make sure their child will have a starting position?

Some children are lacking fervor, and they struggle with negativity. They want to blame their positions in life on anyone or anything. They believe life has not dealt them fair hands. They may struggle with the way they look or a lack of money, or believe they were not blessed with natural abilities. They may be embarrassed about where they live, have difficulty getting along with friends, or become angry with an unfair coach or a teacher. Many kids, after taking a few hard knocks, believe nothing has ever gone right for them, and they don't see any possibility for change in the future. They can get themselves into such a "funk" that they lose all hope. Soon these kids have no motivation to discover anything good about themselves.

A parent can help in this situation by recognizing the negativity that comes from within. Too many negative voices inside their heads will kill creativity.

Jan Graham, an attorney in Salt Lake City, wrote her dissertation on something called "Locus of Control." Locus of Control is a psychological measure of whether an individual believes that the course of his or her life will be determined by internal or external forces. Her subjects were fifth graders.

People who score high on internal locus of control tend to believe their destiny is in their own hands. People who score high on external locus of control tend to believe other people or events will determine the quality of their future.

"High internals" tend to score high on self-esteem tests, do well in school, and rely less on the opinions of others than do "high externals."

Girls who are "high externals" tend to be concerned with their appearance and are highly dependent on the opinions of others. If asked to complete the sentence, "I will be successful in my life if . . . ," high externals pick phrases like "other people like me" or "I marry a successful man." Ouch.

High internals finish the sentence with phrases like "I work hard," "I believe in myself, " and "I stick to my values."

After the data were collected, I was allowed to just hang with the students and observe their interaction. At one school, it took about 30 seconds to see who the leader was. Jenny's classmates, boys and girls, deferred to her. She was team captain every time at every game. She was kind and fair to the other kids . . .

Her score was off-the-chart "internal." She finished the sentence beginning "I will be successful in my life if . . ." with the phrase, "I achieve my goals and am kind to other people." Wow. . . .

What a contrast to current patterns of girls age eight or nine with their tight skirts and pants pushed down as low as possible, breasts pushed [high] . . . The focus for these "tweens" (kids between early childhood and teen years) is entirely the opinion of others.[2]

How do you establish "high internals" within your child? When a child feels the world is against her, you need to, first, sympathize with her; second, love her; and finally, drill into her head this quote: "Bloom where you are planted."

Everyone has been given his own set of challenges to overcome. This needs to be explained again and again throughout your child's life, so give him examples. Point out to your child that he is not alone in his difficulties. No one can change where he was born or what his lot in life shall be, but it is always possible to improve upon it.

Who Knew I Could Play?

Ben loved to play competitive sports. His favorite sport was basketball. He spent hours shooting hoops with whomever he could find. He made the junior high school team and was invited to play up with the high school varsity team. Unfortunately, Ben and his family were involved in a car accident while on summer vacation. Ben was not wearing a seat belt and was thrown from the car. He broke his femur in two places. Even with multiple surgeries and a metal rod, Ben's athletic performance was never the same. Discouragement set in, and Ben lost much of the enthusiasm he had for life. Ben's parents tried everything they could think of to cheer him up, but they too were distressed over the sadness in Ben's face. One day, while immobilizing his leg with ice, Ben picked up his brother's guitar. He strummed a few chords and soon plucked out the melody of a song he had heard on the radio. Ben spent many hours that summer with the guitar. It became his only source of joy. With each agonizing visit to the doctor's office, Ben would raise his spirits by playing the guitar. He asked his parents if he could take a few lessons. Ben soon began to realize that he could play. He took the dedication and love he had found for basketball and focused it on his music. Soon, he was performing his own songs at high school assemblies and local concerts. Ben is now pursuing a music career, one that he loves.

Every child will have challenges. As parents, it is important to compliment a child when she survives a challenge. Gently point out to her the lesson or strength she has learned in the process. If your child is involved in sports, you will have plenty of opportunities to show her the strengths gained from a loss. Michael Jordan emphasizes the power gained in losing:

> I've missed more than 9000 shots in my career. I've lost
> almost 300 games. Twenty-six times I have been trusted
> to take the game winning shot and missed. I've failed over
> and over again in my life—and that is why I succeed.[3]

At the age of fourteen, following his passions, Douglas Barry asked for advice from chief executives from Fortune 500 companies. He compiled this advice in his book, *Wisdom for a Young CEO*. Barry expected serious advice emphasizing ambition.

Instead, the CEOs all mentioned passion, vision, and curiosity as important steps to success. Barry claimed that writing this book taught him that the people in his book were successful because they followed what they loved doing, not because they were exceptionally bright or ambitious. They had the integrity to gain people's trust and shared a vision other people could follow.

Have fun helping your child discover his talents. If you let it, this can be one of the most exciting aspects of parenthood. Enjoy every facet of getting to know more about this complex individual. Here is a little encouragement to let our own creativity shine from Marianne Williamson:

> Our deepest fear is not that we are inadequate. Our
> deepest fear is that we are powerful beyond measure. It
> is our light, not our darkness, that most frightens us. We
> ask ourselves, Who am I to be brilliant, gorgeous, talented,
> fabulous? Actually, who are you not to be? You are a child
> of God. Your playing small does not serve the world.
> There's nothing enlightened about shrinking so that other

people won't feel insecure about you. We are all meant to shine, as children do. We were born to make manifest the glory of God that is within us. It's not just in some of us; it is in everyone, and as we let our own light shine, we unconsciously give others permission to do the same. As we are liberated from our own fear, our presence automatically liberates others.[4]

CHAPTER TWELVE

Taking Time

"To every thing there is a season, and a time to every
purpose under the heaven: A time to be born, and a time
to die; a time to plant, and a time to pluck up that which is
planted; . . . A time to weep, and a time to laugh; a time to
mourn, and a time to dance; . . . for there is a time . . . for
every purpose and for every work."

—Ecclesiastes 3:1–2, 4, 17

The accelerating pace of society is not only hurting our health—it is destroying our families. A balanced life of work and play is necessary to
stay in touch with who we are and what our families are all about.

When life becomes too busy, it is hard to enjoy anything. As a parent,
when you are in a constant rush, it takes away the opportunity to get to know
the people around you—your family. You cannot effectively parent if you are
always in a hurry, accomplishing task after task. It is imperative to put the
brakes on and slow down. You must remember that children would much
rather have your time than your money.

171

Finding time is difficult. It will take some ingenuity on your part, such as realigning your goals and readjusting your priorities, but your health and family are worth it. Here are a few suggestions:

1. *Work Less.* You may not be able to quit your job, but maybe it is possible to cut back on the number of hours.

2. *Kill Distractions.* Shut off the television, the phones, and the computer. Spend time playing and relaxing together. Focus on family.

3. *Let It Go.* It is impossible to finish every task today. Cut yourself some slack and do only the necessary tasks.

4. *Reevaluate.* Get rid of the lessons and activities that you can do without—especially the ones that send you driving across town at rush hour.

Time is a very personal issue. I can give you many suggestions on ways to find more of it, but what it really takes is a commitment for you to decelerate. I realized the importance for change in my own family while attending a little league football game.

That particular game day, it was my responsibility to drive the team players to the football game. We were asked to arrive an hour before the game was to begin so the boys would have time to warm up. It had been a busy day, and I was running behind schedule. I was stressed and in a hurry to pick up each individual boy and get him to the game field on time. Once we made it to the field, I realized I had forgotten my cell phone and laptop. This football field was all the way across town, too great of a distance to run home and grab whatever I needed to keep myself busy. There was nothing to do but observe what was going on around me.

It was a late afternoon game. I noticed that many of the opposing team members were from Polynesian families. I immediately noticed the atmosphere around these families was different from the families on our team.

Entire families arrived together. They were setting up for an early evening barbeque. While they prepared the food, they were laughing and talking with their children, thoroughly enjoying themselves. It was entertaining and relaxing just to watch. As the football game began, they wandered to the sidelines and began cheering on their kids.

What a difference as I watched the parents of our team arrive, directly from work. They looked stressed, with their dress shirts buttoned tightly, their ties constricting their necks. Parents hurried to the sidelines with intense looks upon their faces, upset they had arrived too late for the kickoff. Soon they were pacing up and down the sidelines, tugging at their ties and hollering at their kid and the referees while simultaneously conversing on their cell phones.

Watching this scenario brought a smile to my face. What crazy things we do to ourselves. Watching the Polynesian families made me take stock of the way I was living my life. Running around highly stressed is no way to live, no matter how much money you can make. After watching and comparing both groups of parents, it was easy to acknowledge which families knew how to enjoy time together. I knew something in my own life had to change. What fun is it to go through life always stressed and in a hurry?

It is impossible to parent effectively when you are highly stressed. Once I was able to slow down, I found new value and balance to life. Now that I have adjusted, I will never go back to the stressful life I once lived. As Eddie Cantor said, "Slow down and enjoy life. It's not only the scenery you miss by going too fast—you also miss the sense of where you are going and why."[1]

Take the time to enjoy your children. This short period in their lives will be over quickly. Use this season to talk, to listen, to learn, and to grow together. Gordon B. Hinkley said:

> My plea—and I wish I were more eloquent in voicing
> it—is a plea to save the children. Too many of them walk
> with pain and fear, in loneliness and despair. Children
> need sunlight. They need happiness. They need love and

nurture. They need kindness and refreshment and affection. Every home, regardless of the cost of the house, can provide an environment of love which will be an environment of salvation.[2]

Taking a Little R&R

Going right along with giving yourself more time is allowing yourself to relax. We often do not relax because we are programmed to keep mental checklists. In our own minds, we are not productive unless we are accomplishing the tasks on our lists. Isn't it silly that these checklists could be destroying our families? Ask yourself, "Is my family slowly disintegrating because we are trying to live life at too rapid a pace?" This evaluation process may be the catalyst for a positive change.

In an interview, Reverend Tim Kimmel describes seven flawed family models from his book *Little House on the Freeway*:

- **The Blurred Family:** These families try to relax—constantly—but they can't seem to manage it. They battle with monstrous schedules that would be worthy opponents for King Kong. . . .
- **The Noisy Family:** It cannot stand quiet. A common danger sign—more than one television or stereo is turned on at a time. . . . "Their bodies slumber, but their spirits do not rest," writes Kimmel. "As their hearts cry out for rest, they answer back with entertainment."
- **The New-and-Improved Family:** It's always upgrading its electronic equipment or yard or living room or whatever. . . . "Contentment is always just around the corner—in the latest shipment from L.L. Bean, in being the first one on their block to have one. One what? It doesn't really matter, as long as they're first."
- **The Stealth Family:** The final product of a culture that has tried to ditch right and wrong. The parents are never sure what to teach the

kids because they aren't sure what they believe themselves. Their projects remain unfinished. Ditto for their commitments. Which church will it be this year? Members of these families are not sure they believe in guilt. But they feel it.

- **The Penitent Family:** Suffering servants who die for everybody else's sins. They seek approval through effort. Everyone needs them. No one wants to be like them. They are, Kimmel notes, "quick to sympathize, ready to sacrifice. . . . They have time to nurture everyone else's marriage and family life except their own."

- **The Worried Family:** Nice people, but so fragile and afraid. Often the parents grew up in homes shattered by divorce. Now they fear it will happen to them. They are held hostage by a lack of confidence.

- **The Super Family:** It's only as good as its latest report cards or athletic scores. The father may be absent due to work. Ditto for the mother, except she will work even harder to get the kids to their activities. "They push themselves and their children from one victory to the next. . . . They are a family with much pride, but little joy."[3]

Do any of these families compare with what exists in your home? Slow down and take a look at your life. Learn how to relax and enjoy your family. Multitasking is a wonderful trait we as parents have adapted into our lives out of necessity, but it can be dangerous. How often do you find yourself trying to focus on numerous tasks while simultaneously listening to your children? Unfortunately, we are using this complex gift to destroy our health and happiness. The warning signs of our constant on-the-go lifestyle include high blood pressure, heart attacks, and strokes. Relax. Read a book. Chat with a neighbor. Life was meant to be enjoyed. The mile-long "things to do" list is not going anywhere. It will be there when you are done doing nothing.

Learning how to be idle is difficult. Our forefathers worked hard to survive. We are the direct descendants of generations raised with the philosophy that "idle hands are the devil's workshop." It is not easy to slow down because we receive numerous accolades from constant work in the form of pay raises, promotions, and good old pats on the back from our superiors. The sad truth is that this is no way to live life. Our internal pendulums have swung a little too far towards productivity. We need to make time to discover the quiet center that resides inside of each one of us.

If it is difficult for you to spend time doing nothing, think of it as quality time resting your brain. You will be amazed at the blasts of creativity that occur when you are in a state of calm. Did you know that J.K. Rowling came up with the *Harry Potter* series while relaxing on a train? Have you heard that Newton came up with the law of gravity as he lay on the ground watching an apple fall from a tree to the earth?

Your children will not be around forever, so do not wait for your scheduled two-week vacation to spend time relaxing. Do it every day. Make sure you take the time to enjoy your kids while they are still close in proximity. Lie in the grass and watch the clouds float. Fry an egg on the sidewalk when temperatures rise above 100 degrees. Climb a tree. Discover a four-leaf clover. This free time you are allowing yourself to share with your children is not going to waste. Simply put, you are investing in your relationship.

There was a conference on children and television at the White House, the East room. The Clintons and the Gores were there. We all sat at this huge rectangular table. Different people were asked to present short thoughts. I guess mine was about seven or eight minutes. But for one of those minutes I gave a minute of silence. And when I was going out of the room I heard this voice say, "Thank you, Mister Rogers." I turned. It was one of the military guards, dressed in white and gold. I said, "For what?" He said, "For the silence." I said, "Who did you think about?" He said, "I hadn't thought about him in a long time, but I thought about my grandfather's brother who, just before he died, took me to his basement and gave me his fishing pole. I've loved fishing all my life, and that silence reminded me of that today."[4]

CHAPTER THIRTEEN

~~~

The Best Kind of Example

"Each day of our lives we make deposits in the memory
banks of our children." —Charles R. Swindoll[1]

Parents are continuously under scrutiny by their children. Although children rarely say anything about their parents' lifestyles, they are far more sensitive to them than most of us acknowledge.

Children are taught more from our examples than from what we, as parents, preach. They are constantly monitoring our expressions and moods. Those moods will often be used as a lifeline. A child's attitude about life is affected by the happiness of his parents. His approaches toward education, marriage, employment, and other aspects of life are influenced by what he has witnessed at home. If you view the glass as half empty instead of half full, that is how your child will view it. From that wondrous source, parenting, flows everything a child needs to survive: food, warmth, money, and attitude. Family therapist Jo Ann Larsen tells us this observation begins at birth:

Babies come into this world without a sense of self, though that "self" begins almost immediately to be filled in their parents. Parents become crucial mirrors of their children's worth. . . . Speaking to parents, Dorothy Briggs, author of *Your Child's Self-Esteem*, observes, "Your reflections of him are the first he experiences. To the young child, you are magnified until you take on the appearance of a god."[2]

Now that is pressure—to appear godlike to your child. It does put into perspective the power of example.

The old saying "an apple doesn't fall too far from the tree" holds true. It is through your example and your own thirst for knowledge that your children will seek education. Your children develop skills of serving others from watching you give of yourself. The chance of having a successful marriage is much more probable if your parents are still together. Most likely, they will discipline their children—your grandchildren—the same way you disciplined them.

I am a true believer that what you do, your children will do. Children have been observing their parents since birth—even though children would probably prefer not to admit how many things they do mimic their parents. The inflections in their voice are similar, the way they walk is the same, and you can find similarities even in the way thoughts are processed. I have heard school teachers mention if they are struggling to understand one of their students, when parent/teacher conferences roll around and they meet the parents, everything makes sense.

Recently, I watched as my four-year-old grandson decided his eighteen-month-old brother had broken a rule by stepping into the street. He gently put his arm around him and guided him over to a place on the grass. He sat him down and explained that if he went into the road, he might get hit by a car. Then he said, "I am going to put you in a time out so you can think about it." He then walked away for a minute, came back, and hugged his younger brother, and said "The time out is over. You can play, but not in the street."

Where did a four-year-old learn this behavior? I am quite sure it was from his parents. They probably had no idea how much he had learned from them. These simple moments of example happen every day. I was so proud of my grandsons, my daughter-in-law and my son.

Although at times this example concept is overwhelming, it should help you realize that you have great power over the negative influences that present themselves to your child. At times in their lives, your children will become enamored with people or things that are not worthy of their attention, and that is when they will need a solid example to pull them through. Sportswriter Gordon Monson explains who should be our kids' role models in his article "Misplaced Role Models Disappoint," written in light of sexual assault allegations against Kobe Bryant in 2003.

> This column isn't about Kobe. It's about you. Us. Not about the people we mistakenly put up on a pedestal. Just the ridiculous fact that we put them there in the first place. . . .
>
> Kobe, the buoyant basketball great with the scrubbed-clean image, a fist full of NBA championship rings, and millions of youngsters and adults who idolize him, who have turned him into that which few athletes should be: a role model.
>
> A hero-hungry society incorrectly assigns virtue to celebrity, goodness to clutch performance, particularly when the outer edges seem upright. The uncomfortable fact is, comprehensively speaking, athletes are held up by the public as something more than they are.
>
> They can shoot the lights out. They can hammer dunk. They can thread the needle downfield. They can run and hit like bad mothers. They can drive pitches 500 feet. But they cannot raise our children. They cannot develop our children's character, nor our own. They cannot teach us right from wrong. . . .

Before his retirement, John Stockton spoke accurately about athletes and role modeling: "The real responsibility falls on parents. I can go speak until I'm blue in the face . . . If a parent isn't doing the right things, it won't work. Parenting is a 24-hour-a-day job." . . .

In reality, athletes are not heroes. They are just athletes. Well-known and well-paid or not, they should not be honored, and held to a higher standard, no more than anyone of any other profession. . . . There should be no worship in sports. . . . Kobe is either guilty or not. Either way, he's only a role model if we allow him to be.[3]

These days, it seems more often than not that our children are thrown into situations where the adults could be positive examples, but they are not. As a parent, it is important to acknowledge with your child when an adult is treating him unfairly. You never want to let another adult destroy your child's self-confidence. When they are young and innocent, it will be hard for children to comprehend the negative influence an adult might inflict. At times, we would like to protect our children, but we cannot take away something beneficial from them just because the adults involved are horrible examples.

Participation in sports has the potential of teaching children how to work hard, learn dedication, and understand the importance of teamwork. Unfortunately, there is far too much emphasis placed upon winning, especially from the examples of coaches and parents. If you win, you are considered successful, a champion. If you lose, you hang your head, act discouraged, and slither away. How sad is this concept? Unfortunately, it is often encouraged by adult coaches.

In every situation possible, find the hero so your child won't lose faith in the adults in her life. Fred Engh has tried to do some good in the world of youth athletics. Use Fred and this article, "Playing it Safe" by Marianne Bhonslay, as an example for your children the next time you have to explain the negative influence of another adult.

Fred Engh has seen it a million times. Little League coaches managing ten-year-olds as if it were the seventh game of the World Series. Twelve-year-old kids running through soccer drills with the demands and stress of preparing for the World Cup. The culprit? Over-zealous coaches. Parents living vicariously through the athletic triumphs—and failures—of their children.

"It's rampant across America," says Engh, the president, CEO, and founder of the National Youth Sports Coaches Association. "I watched a baseball game where a nine-year-old was on the mound, in tears, holding his elbow and telling the coach—who was also his Dad—that his arm hurt," Engh recounts. "The father responded, 'Son, this is a man's game. You get in there and pitch.'"

Winning games and championships often comes at the expense of kids getting a fair shot of playing time, and often verbal and occasionally physical abuse of kids who are not "performing" up to coaching's unrealistic and unwarranted expectations. Somebody has got to do something about this . . . We have to eliminate the "win at any cost attitude."

By age thirteen, Engh continues, as many as 70 percent of 20 million [kids participating in youth leagues] will drop out of their local or recreational youth leagues. Engh wanted answers. As a former elementary physical education instructor and a high school coach and athletic director, he found them.

"Sports are a part of our culture, but what about kids who are being thrust into a major league attitude before they've actually learned the physical motor skills? I began to see inequities." He set out to rectify them. Engh banked his career and personal finances on his belief that "coaches working with children shouldn't be working with them without training." He set up the NYSCA, and its prime focus was "to make sports fun."

Coaches take clinics in sports medicine and sports psychology and are required to abide by a strict code of ethics. To qualify for NYSCA membership, volunteer coaches complete a first-year certification clinic and pay the annual $15 fee. The NYSCA's ethical code requires coaches to follow nine rules, presented with the authority of the ten commandments. [These include] placing the emotional and physical well-being of players ahead of any personal desire to win; promising to lead by example in demonstrating fair play and sportsmanship; and promising to provide a safe playing situation for players. "Coaches have a tremendous influence on kids," says Engh. "Two thousand years ago, Plato said it best," says Engh quoting a favorite scholar. "A child is at his learning best when at play." Engh abides by the Margaret Mead slogan he has posted above the NYSCA's front entrance. It reads, Engh quotes, "Never doubt that a small group of committed people can change the world. They are, in fact, the only ones that ever have."[4]

You can never rely on other adults to be the role models for your children. The only guaranteed example you have is yourself, so be a first-class example: "As ye sow, so shall ye reap."

CHAPTER FOURTEEN

The "D" Word

"A soft answer turneth away wrath: but grievous words stir
up anger." —*Proverbs 15:1*

Did you know that the word *discipline* comes from the Latin word
disciplina, which means "to teach" or "to learn"? Discipline was never
designed to be a form of punishment.

If you have created a Safe Haven, built strong relationships, realigned
your ideals, understood your belief windows, changed your behavior
towards your child, stopped using control, honored your child's rights, protected motivation, become involved in education, promoted their creativity,
and loved and accepted your child, *there will be no need for discipline.*

If you find yourself relying on discipline as punishment, something is
wrong. It is time to re-evaluate. When in the thick of family matters, sometimes it is difficult to clearly understand where you might be making mistakes. Now is a good time to enlist the help of an outsider, like a friend or

therapist. Choose someone who will give you honest feedback—someone who will tell you directly if your belief windows are foggy.

This chapter is purposefully short because discipline should no longer be necessary.

CHAPTER FIFTEEN

Now Make It So

Once there was a great kingdom. This kingdom was known throughout the land for its beauty, but through time, all that had changed. Now the once great buildings were falling down and in need of repair. The farms were now small and did not grow enough food for the kingdom. The king of this land did not look as you might expect a king to look, for he did not have a magnificent throne or flowing robes. He was the king of a poor kingdom, so he looked quite ordinary and poor himself.

One day, as the king sat down to a meager dinner of bread and a slab of cheese, there came a knock at the castle door. The king's servant opened the door to find an old man with a large oak walking stick.

"Hail," said the old man. "I am but passing through your

kingdom, and I am looking for an inn to spend the night in."

The servant frowned. "This is not an inn. This is the king's castle."

The traveler looked around in surprise. "This is not much of a castle," he said.

"Aye," the servant agreed.

"Still, I am weary from my journey. I would like to rest here."

"You must inquire of my lord," the servant said.

"Lead me to him," said the old man.

The servant led the old man down a dark, cold hallway to the king's dining room.

"You are the king of this land?" the old man asked.

"I am," the king replied.

"You do not look like a king."

The king frowned. "I am the king of a poor kingdom. We were once a great kingdom, but all that has changed."

The old man nodded slowly. "Why do you not change back?" he asked.

"*Change*?" the king replied angrily. "We have tried, only to fail."

"You lack one thing," said the old man. "If you will give me supper and lodging for the night, I will show you why you fail." The king looked at him thoughtfully then said, motioning to the platter of bread and cheese, "Eat your fill."

The next morning, the old man came to the king in his throne room. "You have lived up to your part of the bargain," he said. "Now I will live up to mine. Follow me."

The king followed the old man to the castle balcony. There, the old man brought out a long, round canister and pulled from it a brass tube, a spyglass. He raised the spyglass to his eye and looked out over the land until a smile crossed his face. Then he handed the spyglass to the king. "Look thither."

The king looked out through the glass. He could see great farms and gardens, magnificent castles and cathedrals.

"You are a wizard," said the king. "It is a trick of the glass."

"It is no trick," said the old man. But when the king put down the glass his kingdom looked the same as before. "Nothing has changed."

"No," said the old man. "Change requires work. But one must first see before doing." The king again raised the glass. "What greatness this kingdom holds. You have seen what might be," said the old man. "Now go and make it so. After two harvests, I will return for my spyglass."

The king, on horseback, went out into his kingdom. He rode until he came to the edge of a once beautiful garden, now overrun with weeds and thistles. A group of villagers was standing outside its fence.

"Why do you not use the garden?" the king asked them.

"It is not fit, sire," replied a woman.

"So it is not," agreed the king. "But it could be. Look." The king held out the spyglass. One by one, the villagers looked through the tube at the garden. The weeds and thistles were gone, and the lawns were lush and inviting. But when they set down the glass, the garden had returned to its overgrown state.

"It is an amusing device," said one man. "But of no use."

"No use, indeed," the king said. "Behold, knave." He

went to the garden and began to pull the weeds up by his own hand. When the villagers saw what he was doing, they too began to pull up weeds until they had uncovered a large marble statue of an angel. The people stared at the statue in silent awe. At length, the king mounted his horse. Before he left, he said, "You have seen what might be. Now make it so."

This story has been passed down in my family as a reminder that our lives will not often go as envisioned. My parents emphasized that hard work and a good attitude go a long way to change or improve whatever challenges you incur.

I hope I have given you an idea of what your homes can be. Creating the Safe Haven will change your life and that of your family forever. If you begin pulling the weeds to uncover the beauty, your family will soon join with you.

Allow yourself to change, to improve. We are shaped and fashioned by what we love. It is possible to learn more from your children than they learn from you.

Be gentle on yourself. As parents, we all stumble, every one of us. Be kind to yourself as you and your children struggle toward creating better relationships. Perfection takes time. One person cannot parent alone, so ask for help. It is much easier to fix your parenting by helping one another. Be patient with yourself. We are all trying to do our best. I leave you with the words of Gordon B. Hinckley:

> You have nothing in this world more precious than your children. When you grow old, when your hair turns white and your body grows weary, when you are prone to sit in a rocker and meditate on the things of your life, nothing will be so important as the question of how your children have turned out. It will not be the money you have made. It will not be the cars you have owned. It will not be the large

house in which you live. The searing question that will cross your mind again and again will be, *How well have my children done?*

If the answer is that they have done very well, then your happiness will be complete. If they have done less than well, then no other satisfaction can compensate for your loss.[1]

Sources

Introduction

1. Hinckley, Gordon B. "Walking in the Light of the Lord." *Ensign* Nov. 1998: Print.

Chapter 1: Safe Haven

1. "Text of Mrs. Bush's Speech." *The Washington Post* (pre-1997 Fulltext): 0. Jun 02 1990. Web.

2. Berret, Michael E., PhD. "Team Up for Teens: Guidelines for Treating Adolescents with Eating Disorders." *Center for Change* May 2002. Web.

3. Good Reads. Goodreads, Inc. Last modified 2014. Web.

4. WylieBlog. http://wylie.blogspot.com/2003_02_23_archive.html

5. Duncan, Stephen F. "Subduing the Spirit of Contention." *BYU Magazine* Spring 2004: Print.

6. Warner, C. Terry. *Bonds That Make Us Free: Healing Our Relationships, Coming to Ourselves.* Arbinger Institute, 2001. Print.

7. Andreas, Connierae and Tamara Andreas. *Core Transformation.* Real People Press, 1994. Print.

8. Chopra, Deepak. *Ageless Body, Timeless Mind: The Quantum Alternative to Growing Old.* New York: Harmony Books, 1993. Print.

Chapter 2: Building Relationships

1. Johnson, Spencer, MD. *The One Minute Father.* New York: Candle Communications Corporation, 1983. Print.

Chapter 3: Understanding Ideals

1. Young, Colin. "Hey, Parents . . . Your Kid Sucks." *Baseball Perspective.* Blogger, 30 April 2013. Web.

2. Chopra, Deepak. *Ageless Body, Timeless Mind: The Quantum Alternative to Growing Old.* New York: Harmony Books, 1993. Print.

3. Lewis, C.S. *Mere Christianity.* New York: Harper Collins, 1980. Print.

4. Smith, Hyrum W. *Pain Is Inevitable, Misery Is Optional.* Salt Lake City: Deseret Book, 2004. Print.

5. Cameron, Julia. *The Artist's Way: A Spiritual Path to Higher Creativity.* New York: Putnam Book, 1992. Print.

Chapter 4: Behavior

1. Hartmann, Tom. *Attention Deficit Disorder: A Different Perception.* 2nd ed. Mythical Intelligence, 1997. Print.

2. Hartmann, Tom. *Beyond ADD.* Grass Valley, CA: Mythical Intelligence, 1996. Print.

3. Cameron, Julia. *The Artist's Way: A Spiritual Path to Higher Creativity.* New York: Putnam Book, 1992. Print.

4. Shoshanah Shear. "Children Live What They Learn—Poem by Dorothy

Law Nolte." *Healing Occupational Therapy*. Blogger, 5 June 2011. Web.

5. Bombeck, Erma. "The Grooming of Domestic Perfectionists." *The Free Lance-Star* 3 Nov 1989, 23. Print.

6. "When Children Lie." *Better Homes and Gardens*. Meredith Corporation, 2014. Web.

7. Lee, Harold B. "My Daughter Prepares for Marriage." *Relief Society Magazine* June 1955: 348-49. Print.

Chapter 5: Control

1. Chopra, Deepak. *Ageless Body, Timeless Mind: The Quantum Alternative to Growing Old*. New York: Harmony Books, 1993. Print.

2. Locke, Michelle. "Controversy Over 'Tough-Love' Camp." *Associated Press* 5 Jan 1998. Print.

3. Silverstein, Olga and Beth Rashbaum. *The Courage to Raise Good Men*. New York: Viking, 1994. Print.

4. Fields, Jennifer. "Alan Ross, Suicide Hotline Director." *The Oprah Magazine*. May 2001: 243. Print.

5. Mullen, Holly. "An Understanding Adult Can Make All the Difference in a Troubled Teen's Life." *Salt Lake Tribune* 28 Jan 2003. Print.

6. Larsen, Jo Ann, D.S.W. "Don't Let Issue of Control Spoil Relationships." *Deseret News* 17 May 1992. Print.

7. Larsen, Jo Ann, D.S.W. "'Annual Review' Can Keep Marriage Healthy." *Deseret News* 18 Aug 1991: 12. Print.

8. Kirby, Robert. "When Junior Leaves, Don't Make It Worse." *Salt Lake Tribune* 11 May 2002. Print.

Chapter 6: Motivation

1. Cameron, Julia. *The Artist's Way: A Spiritual Path to Higher Creativity*. New York: Putnam Book, 1992. Print.

2. Welsh, Patrick. "Never Good Enough: Parents Do No Favors By Expecting Far Too Much." *The Washington Post* 28 Nov 1999: B01. Print.

3. Morrison, Toni. *Sula*. New York: Penguin Books, 1973. Print.

4. Tanner, John S. "Amateurism and Excellence." *BYU Magazine* Winter 2005. Print.

5. Monson, Gordon. "Positively Mental." *The Salt Lake Tribune* 4 July 2002: D1. Print.

6. Bala, Gary. "Book Excerpts: Arthur Ashe on Tennis." *Essential Tennis* 19 March 2010. Web.

7. Monson, Gordon. "14 Years Later, Hornacek Has Made the Most of Trip from Obscurity." *The Salt Lake Tribune* 20 April 2000: E9. Print.

8. Good Reads. Goodreads, Inc. Last modified 2014. Web.

9. "Thomas Edison." *Wikiquote*. Wikimedia, 16 Feb. 2014. Web.

10. Kelly, Brian C. *Best Little Stories from the Life and Times of Winston Churchill*. Nashville, TN: Cumberland House Publishing, 2008. Print.

11. Brothers, Dr. Joyce. "When a Dream Doesn't Come True." *Parade Magazine* March 2002. Print.

Chapter 7: Education

1. Hartmann, Tom. *Beyond ADD*. Grass Valley, CA: Mythical Intelligence, 1996

2. Robinson, Holly. "Are We Raising Boys Wrong?" *Ladies Home Journal* Nov. 1998: 96–100. Print.

3. Sowell, Thomas. "'Good' Teachers." *The Thomas Sowell Reader*. New York: Basic Books, 2011. Print.

4. Faughum, Robert. *All I Really Need to Know I Learned in Kindergarten*. New York: Ballentine Books, 2003. Print.

Chapter 8: Teenagers

1. Kutner, Lawrence, PhD. "You Can Make a Difference." *Peer Pressure and Smoking*. Phillip Morris USA, 2005. Print.

2. Clement, C. Ross. "Talking With Teens." *Ensign* June 2005: 32. Print.

3. Rubiner, Betsy. "Combatting Popular Kids and Their Cliques." *Better Homes and Gardens* March 2004: 148. Print.

Chapter 9: Teaching Your Child

1. Cortez, Marjorie. "Follow Parents' Lead is Good Advice for Today." *Deseret News* 2 Nov. 2002. Print.

2. Kikuchi, Yoshikhilo. "Broken Windows, Broken Hearts." *Ensign* April 2004: 8. Print.

3. Hopson, Judi Light, Emma H. Hopson, and Ted Hagen, PhD. "Teaching Kids to Help With Chores." *The Salt Lake Tribune* 1 Dec 2003. Print.

4. McGraw, Phil. "Talking to Your Teen About Sex." *Dr. Phil*. Petestki Productions, n.d. Web.

5. Bombeck, Erma. "Sex Is Instinctive, but Maturity Isn't." *Deseret News* 8 Sept. 1991. Print.

6. Plambeck, Joseph. "Teens Who Are Close to Mothers Delay Having Sex, Report Says." *Knight Ridder News Service* 4 Sept. 2002. Print.

Chapter 10: Thou Shalt Not Judge

1. Welsh, Patrick. "Never Good Enough: Parents Do No Favors By Expecting Far Too Much." *The Washington Post* 28 Nov 1999: B01. Print.

2. Jennings, Marianne M. "Having Average Kids Isn't Such a Bad Thing." *Deseret News* 29 Dec. 1996. Print.

3. Hinckley, Gordon B. *Teachings of Gordon B. Hinckley*. Salt Lake City: Deseret Book, 1997. Print.

Chapter 11: Just Being Yourself

1. Larsen, Jo Ann, D.S.W. "Embrace Change as a Path to Life-Affirming 'Rebirth.'" *Deseret News* 15 Aug 1996. Print.

2. Graham, Jan. "Help Kids Trust Selves, Not Trends." *The Salt Lake Tribune* 13 July 2002. Print.

3. *Competitive Advantage*. Competitive Advantage, 2014. Web.

4. Williamson, Marianne. *A Return to Love: Reflections on the Principles of "A Course in Miracles."* New York: HarperCollins, 1992. Print.

Chapter 12: Taking Time

1. *The Quotations Page*. QuotationsPage, 2013. Web.

2. Hinckley, Gordon B. "Save the Children." *Ensign* Nov 1994. Print.

3. Mattingly, Terry. "Fast-Lane Syndrome Traps Many Families." *Deseret News* 27 July 1992. Print.

4. Zoba, Wendy Murray. "Won't You Be My Neighbor?" *Christianity Today* 6 March 2000. Print.

Chapter 13: The Best Kind of Example

1. Good Reads. Goodreads, Inc. Last modified 2014. Web.

2. Larson, Jo Ann, D.S.W. "Praise Takes a Minute but May Last a Lifetime." *Deseret News* 19 Nov. 1989. Print.

3. Monson, Gordon. "Misplaced Role Models Disappoint." *The Salt Lake Tribune* 20 July 2003. Print.

4. Bhonslay, Marianne. "Playing It Safe." *Team Leader*

Chapter 15: Now Make It So

1. Hinckley, Gordon B. "Your Greatest Challenge, Mother." *Ensign* Oct. 2000. Print.

About the Author

Maggie Stevens graduated with degrees in sociology and youth leadership. Professionally, Maggie works with youth groups, parent groups, and educators offering parenting help to struggling families.

She also volunteers the majority of her time to *The Parent Fix* Foundation, a non-profit organization dedicated to improving family life. She is the proud mother of five children and four grandchildren.

About Familius

Welcome to a place where mothers are celebrated, not compared. Where heart is at the center of our families, and family at the center of our homes. Where boo boos are still kissed, cake beaters are still licked, and mistakes are still okay. Welcome to a place where books—and family—are beautiful. Familius: a book publisher dedicated to helping families be happy.

Visit Our Website: www.familius.com

Our website is a different kind of place. Get inspired, read articles, discover books, watch videos, connect with our family experts, download books and apps and audiobooks, and along the way, discover how values and happy family life go together.

Join Our Family

There are lots of ways to connect with us! Subscribe to our newsletters at www.familius.com to receive uplifting daily inspiration, essays from our Pater Familius, a free ebook every month, and the first word on special discounts and Familius news.

Become an Expert

Familius authors and other established writers interested in helping families be happy are invited to join our family and contribute online content. If you have something important to say on the family, join our expert community by applying at:

www.familius.com/apply-to-become-a-familius-expert

Get Bulk Discounts

If you feel a few friends and family might benefit from what you've read, let us know and we'll be happy to provide you with quantity discounts. Simply email us at specialorders@familius.com.

Website: www.familius.com

Facebook: www.facebook.com/paterfamilius

Twitter: @familiustalk, @paterfamilius1

Pinterest: www.pinterest.com/familius

The most important work

you ever do will be within the

walls of your own home.